The Ancient Key:
A Hidden Secret to Life

Ken Viñales

Copyright © 2019
The Ancient Key
by Ken Viñales.

All rights reserved. No part of this publication may be reproduced, redistributed, or transmitted in any form or by any means, including photocopying, recording, or other electronic or mechanical methods, without the prior written permission of the publisher, except in the case of brief quotations embodied in critical reviews and certain other noncommercial uses permitted by copyright law.

Media Information:
TheRareFew.com **Website**
@Ken_Vinales **Main Instagram**
@VFTransportation – **Business Instagram**
@KenVinales - **Twitter**

ISBN-13: 978-0-9994018-5-9
ISBN-10: 0-9994018-5-8

Please leave a review on Amazon, thank you in advance!

Current Edition: July 2019

Copyright © 2019 Ken Viñales

All rights reserved. No part of this publication may be reproduced, redistributed, or transmitted in any form or by any means, including photocopying, recording, or other electronic or mechanical methods, without the prior written permission of the publisher, except in the case of brief quotations embodied in critical reviews and certain other noncommercial uses permitted by copyright law.

Acknowledgments

Who would've ever thought that we would be here? I want to thank you for believing in me. The beautiful thing about any process is that it can be recreated into something that is even better. My first book, *First in the Family*, was a success, which inspired me to release the second, which happens to be related in a subliminal way. At the time of me writing these words, the world still has yet to discover me. By the time these words reach you, more people will know me, but I know this is only the beginning. You were able to consume my words and energy, before they made the real impact, which will come long after our death! Thank you for believing!

Author's Note

If someone would have told me that I was on the path to becoming one of the greatest writers to ever live, my mind would have been confused. A few months ago, I was in a classroom, wondering if I would be able to find a way to become financially free. Today I am two books in, which I am publishing, marketing, selling and distributing on my own. The point that I am trying to make is that you need to follow your dreams, by any means. You must realize that it only takes one day for your life to change. It may seem strange, but my methods will help people break free from the cage that confines their mind, and help the stars align.

Ken Viñales

Contents

Volume 2

1|	Entrance	1
2|	Concealed	19
3|	Blind Control	29
4|	You-niverse	50
5|	Radiation	62
6|	Imagination	76
7|	Attraction	76
8|	Mastermind	89
9|	Manifestation	99

> "The moment the door to your dreams appear, remove fear and allow God to steer."
>
> -Ken Viñales

1

Entrance

September 1, 2016

Before you can live a part of you has to die. You have to let go of what could have been, how you should have acted and what you wish you would have said differently. When the last chapter of this book was complete, I knew my life would be different, but I was not sure how. The crazy thing about life is that the future has already happened.

What if I told you that you have already lived and died? I am speaking from a time that you have not physically lived. How did I know you would end up here? When you connect with your highest self, it is done through love and purpose. I died inside, to come alive outside. The old me is no longer because the future me has taken over.

What if I told you it was possible to speak things into existence, long before they ever happen? When these words reach you it will be many years later. Allow me to catch you up. Much has changed since the release of this book. I knew this book would touch millions, but I didn't know exactly when or how, but I know why.

Have you ever been sure of something, but fear of being wrong crowded your thoughts? What do you do when you know everyone around you is going to start treating you differently, but they do not know it yet? This story is going to be told for generations because of the endless inspiration.

You were brought to me for a reason. It took many seasons, but great rewards come with obedience. You must obey the laws or you will fall victim to many illusions, that leave you in confusion. There is something different about me. The first cue, is that I have created my own future.

I have found something that only the greats understand. This did not happen by chance, but rather a precise plan. There will be many changes in my life, but just know time is aligning for us to one day meet. Do you know where you are? Look around you. Now wherever you think you are, you are not. What do I mean? I would like to first, welcome you to my dream. It is time that you learn about *The Ancient Key*.

This morning I woke up and I am officially in my dream. Do you know what it is like to have a purpose awakening, convincing you to become the greatest? I am the greatest writer of my generation and I said it before I became it.

How many times per day do you go into your future? Have you ever even went into your future? Do you know how to go into your future? I am not able to tell you how far ahead I am, but just know it is much after you read this book. You still do not believe me when I tell you that we have connected for a reason?

How can you tell the world about something when they cannot see it yet? When you are ahead of your time you have to strategically find a way to reveal it to the world. Coming in last place was no longer an option. One day is going to be your day. My day just so happened to be documented.

When a blessing comes you have to take advantage of it. *The Ancient Key* was a blessing, many doors have opened since releasing it. Those who once doubted me are now confused by what has been accomplished. How surprised would you be if something bigger was in motion?

You are receiving these words because the time has come. This awakening was something that changed the direction of my life, leading me directly to you. Before we met I knew you. I knew you would benefit from my words, that is why this message must be heard.

I would like to explain to you why this information is going to change your life, possibly overnight so you must make sure the decision to continue is right. Do you want to enter? With knowledge comes power. With power comes attention. With attention comes energy.

The crazy thing about life is that we, humans, study other subjects. We study math, science, and history, but when is the last time you've studied yourself? Throughout the years, my past has helped me recreate my future. The first thing that I know about you is that you are a person of growth. You want to grow. You have a dream that you want to achieve and that is why I am here because I believe.

The Present Moment

It is March 1st, 2019 and you are reading these words because it is time. I have been documenting my life for the past five years. For so long, I remained confused about what my future would hold. Now I look back seeing that I have always been in control because I aligned my mind body and soul.

On December 15, 2018, nearly three months ago, I graduated college, with a B.A. in psychology only to publish my first book just a few weeks later. My journey through college led me to a dark place mentally. Before this moment, I was not sure how it was going to come about. In fact, I was not aware that just three months later I would be constructing the second book of this legendary journey.

First in the Family was just the beginning. *First in the Family* was my emergence as the greatest writer of this era. *First in the Family* got my foot in the door. It was the bait that I was hoping people would bite on. You took the bait, now you are here. Are you sure you want to enter? It will require you to remove all fear. What if this changes your perception of the world? What if this changes your perception of yourself? Could you handle leaving behind who you are today?

It was time for our stories to finally align. I found something a few years back. It is what intrigued me to write from a future perspective in the current moment. What if I told you it is what led you to me? I wrote about this moment before it happened, now it's time to write about it as it is happening.

The last three months of my life, have in a way been a movie. What you are about to consume will shift your reality moving forward. Before I reached this moment, I never knew how it would happen. I just knew it would happen. Do you believe in thought power? Creative thinking is spiritual. Many people do not believe in spiritual power, but I will use my own life experiences to explain how my life has transformed, through applying ancient science, wisdom and demonstrate how you can emulate these methods.

When you learn how to control your thoughts with purpose, a transformation occurs in your reality. Many people are living in a tragedy because of their mentality towards reality. The worst thing you can do is think about the things you don't want. What do you think happens when a mind is filled with negativity?

Revisit the Past

I went back many years, traveling through time with my thoughts, allowing me to collect endless wisdom. Wisdom is created when knowledge is applied to an experience. This creates new information for you to access. I have collected much wisdom over the past years, but what good will it do if I don't find a way to give back?

An evolution can only occur when you learn how to grow by giving back. Before stepping into my dreams I had to walk away from my past. In order to achieve great things, fear must be confronted and removed. It is scary to think of the consequences that will come from failure, but why does that matter?

When I entered this dream, it was not done with fear. All my mind knows is go. I take action, without thought, entering every situation with boldness. Entrance is about getting rid of fear and walking with faith. *The Ancient Key* is designed in a scientific way to enhance your mind's perspective of life. The objective is to incorporate what I have learned about the universe, spirituality, psychology and success into my experiences, suggesting that, if these methods are applied right they can change your life night by night.

Predicted our Encounter

Many influencers profit off their audiences by selling them dreams. They cast perceptions that deceive the one who receives. Everything I am claiming, I have done. People have claimed that I am crazy. People have claimed that I am on drugs. The crazy thing is that nothing I am saying is new, but old, from ancient times.

The stars have somehow aligned, opening up several doors in my mind. This strategy will combine real life, with science, which is in a way undeniable. There is a scientific way to enter the mind that only experts like psychologists understand. How did I know we would connect years before you knew of my existence? What if I told you that everything you experienced now was just a part of the plan? What if I told you that the universe was preparing you for me?

One day I woke up with a vision. The vision was of me becoming one of the greatest humans of this era. If your mind conceives, then you can achieve so don't think, just act and your reality will begin to reflect your mentality. Don't hesitate to walk through the door of your dreams, all you have to do is remove fear and allow God to steer. This chapter is called *Entrance* because you must know that indecisiveness is the first step towards failure.

If you are not sure of your destination, why would people follow? What you must understand is that humans are biologically hardwired to follow. In other words, before we are born we are driven to conform. Think about the fastest growing social media app, Instagram. Social media has given us a way to create our own following, but many people think it's luck, but there is a science to influence. Once you learn the science of influence, it will make it easier to manifest goals.

What is Manifestation?

All humans manifest, whether it is consciously or unconsciously. This moment right here is a product of manifestation. Before you lived this moment, I created it with my mind in a different time. If you are reading these words, then the stars have aligned. You must know where your true power resides.

In nine chapters, through a real story, your mind will begin to reprogram itself. Manifestation is a term that is often used, but rarely applied correctly. This story that you are going to read, correlates directly with yours. Most humans have a vision, now you are witnessing the science and power of thought precision.

Many people talk about mind and thought power, but only few apply the most important ingredient. True manifestation comes when you remove fear, suppress thought and take action. The problem with society today, myself at one point is that we talk, plan, research, think, but few of us act, especially with unwavering faith.

Are you aware of what is truly in control? As a human, you must understand who you are, within who you are. Why do you like the things that you like? Why do you gravitate towards the people that you gravitate towards? In chapter three, *Blind Control*, you will discover the secret to unlock the limitless potential inside of you.

Enter with Boldness

The moment you enter your dream, be confident in your ability to achieve what your mind conceives. Before I ever reached this level or began this journey, I knew we would meet. I knew you before you knew me. Now we are here, which can suggest proven destiny. I would like for you to retrace your steps.

What if your past was preparing you for this moment? What if I had the key to unlock your mind, elevating you to your prime? You are now here. I know you are here with a vision. I know you are here with a dream. I know there is something that you want to achieve because I can feel the desire growing in you.

I see things long before they happen. It's as if I've been here before, but people usually don't understand when I come from that type of perspective. So allow me to open up your mind. Allow me to share with you something that no one ever knew. Allow me to share with you why you must chase your dreams.

I woke up one morning, this morning to be exact and realized that my book was in another country, all over the world, in the hands of people whom I've never met before. *First in the Family* is one of the greatest self-help books of this era. Three months later, I am going back into my archives to dig up the book that created this whole moment. *The Ancient Key* is exactly what you need.

At 22 years old, my accomplishments are far beyond my time. People are being changed by my story. People are being changed by my ambition. There were times where I doubted myself. There were times where I didn't know what would happen. For a long time, my life was tragic.

Wisdom is Power

Today many people are asking what changed for me. Those who aren't close to me don't understand the sacrifices I made for this. I am writing another book back to back because this was not luck, but scientific strategy. My life is proof that *The Ancient Key* is what the world needs.

We all have different abilities. My ability is to turn wisdom into stories that connect. There are few people who are able to speak from experience and I am one. I am not one of those marketing gurus who dropped out of college. I went to college, acquired knowledge, while educating myself to build generational wealth.

The turning point for me was understanding the scientific difference between knowledge and wisdom. Knowledge is the transferring of information to your mind. When you read a book you interpret that information as knowledge. When you interact with a teacher, their wisdom becomes knowledge. My wisdom is being interpreted as knowledge.

At one point in time I thought knowledge was power, but allow me to ask you something. If knowledge was as powerful as people claim it to be, wouldn't we all have extreme powers? The common misconception is that consuming, will lead to a great benefit, but that is false. Consumption is only one aspect, the first aspect.

We all have a large bank of knowledge, but the one thing lacking is wisdom. What is wisdom? Wisdom comes with action. Action is the universal key that is required for all the laws discussed. My life changed when I began acting on the information that I was consuming. Applied knowledge equals wisdom, which can transform into power.

Equations for Life

Did you know life can be deduced down to simple equations? Equations don't only apply to math. There are also undeniable equations for life and success. Success is not luck. Success is strategy. The difference maker is learning how to use situations from all time periods to unlock new information. Allow me to use an example for demonstration.

When I began college, I changed my major over four times. I went into a deep depression. My mind was in a very dark place, a place that I don't like entering. Do you know what it is like to feel like you are going to fail at life? Do you know what it is like to fear being average? My mother and brother have both reached high levels of success, but it was not seeming to be the same for my quest.

The pain from regret is stronger than the pain from failure. There was a time where part of me thought my future would consist of average accomplishments. Do you know what it is like to walk without purpose? Your mind is constantly searching for a direction, fearing to face the reflection.

My original goal when entering college was to find a regular job. I thought I would spend my life working for a corporation, not building one, but one day I found something. I found something that I am now giving to you. There are many things that you must understand.

First you must understand that it took me five years just to say that I am beginning. I am just now making an imprint on this big dent. I have big dreams, dreams that are going to take years to achieve, but what I know about time is that it's not real it is just a perception.

Learn to Take Control

What if I told you that the vision in your mind has already happened? Did you know that you have come to me, long before you have come to me. I extended a call into the universe, sending direct signals for those who needed to hear this message. In other words, you have attracted events into your life that would eventually lead you to me.

I have the answers that you have been searching for. I have the answers that you didn't even know you were looking for. Now that I am in my dreams, I am looking back on life knowing that every situation, every encounter, every lesson led up to this moment. Every single situation that you encounter on a daily basis is somehow leading you to me, which will eventually direct you to a higher version of yourself.

I speak on experiences before I live them so walking in them gives me control. I am the one. I am the one who was able to break a generational curse. I am the one who was able to make a name for myself by myself with no help. This is the result of building my wealth stealth.

Rain Drop in Ocean

People often respect those who put in time. People often respect those who come from nothing. I came from nothing. I saw my mother struggle. I saw my father in a cage. When you come from that type of background, you know that the odds are always going to be against you.

Do you know that society wasn't designed for those who grow up in the wrong environment? It is like a rain drop in the ocean, meaning minorities often have very few options. The influence of it is so powerful, like a rain drop in an ocean, that individuals get sucked in, without knowing that they were born to actually win. An environment can be so powerful that according to evolution, different species have been created because of the different environmental pressures, causing traits to emerge that were not previously existent, over millions of years.

Connect with Old Minds

For the four years, I spent in college all I did was study the minds of wealthy men. Psychology and sociology interest me because it gives me a deep insight on the mind that controls us. If you don't understand who you are at the root, then you can turn into someone you never knew.

The dream is not the goal. The dream is not the material. The dream is the process that it takes to get there. Before I made a dollar using my gifts, thousands of hours were invested into the vision.

I was trying to figure out a way to increase my power. How do you increase your power? The key is to digest as much wisdom as possible. What's the requirement after that? You come up with a plan. Have you taken the time to write out a detailed plan for the next five years, that is clear to the ear?

Entering your dreams is not about reception. You should not desire to receive anything in the beginning because the craft is always more important than the money. Once the knowledge is acquired, action must be taken. Action is the underlying foundation that your life must be built upon.

The more you act, the more wisdom will be gained. After a plan is created it won't serve any purpose if it is not pursued. That's how increase your wisdom. I'm only 22, but my wisdom is timeless. I have experienced many things that some people never do. My journey is a sign that my purpose is coming from truth.

Awaken Greatness Within

I am releasing two books, *First in the Family* and *The Ancient Key*, back to back because I want to show you that the universe is alive. *First in the Family* was the emergence. *The Ancient Key* is the statement. There are laws to this universe that you have not been taught about. My life is a testimony. This is the power of a purpose awakening, which originated from enhanced awareness.

I want you to know something. It doesn't matter where you come from. It doesn't matter what your parents have been through. It doesn't matter what anyone says about you. The only thing that matters is the limitations you create for your mind. In other words, before taking action you must program your mind through suggestion, affirmations and commands.

Programing is the essential tool, which will help build your vision even more. You see, I look into my future every day because I know every day my future life is being created. I know every day my thoughts are being sent out into the universe. There are many secrets to the *You-niverse*, which we will discuss in chapter 4. What if I had information that could change your life overnight, if applied right?

The Computer Analogy

Humans resemble computers. We're like computers in the sense that we can program our mind to act in certain ways. Action is the underlying foundation, but if action isn't taken in the right direction, then progress will not be made. The foundation must be built upon something. You must build your foundation with affirmations.

The secret to taking control of your mind is by giving it a specific direction, with words and controlled thoughts. It is what keeps you on a constant level day in and day out. Things are going to come at you. Obstacles will deter you. Once you understand the two entities that exist within you, a completely different world will open up.

The only reality is perception, which means we can program our mind to only see greatness. We can program our mind, embedding emotions, to create actions that originate from desire and love, which I will break down in chapter 5, *Radiation*. Emotions are important to understand for a variety of reasons.

Many people questioned my decision to study psychology. During the process, no one understood what the result would lead to except for me. Thoughts create emotions, emotions create actions and actions lead to results. At a young age, on a unconscious level, we associate feelings with actions. In other words, if we are unconscious to a negative embedding, then we will always act out of that negative emotion, which will lead to negative decisions in the outside world.

Awareness is what awakens you. Programming plus reflection heightens awareness. There is a vision in your mind. The reason you must find a way is because there is someone depending on your story for inspiration. What if you were destined to become one of the greatest? Would you run away or would you take it?

We receive ideas for a reason. If you search through ancient wisdom, connecting with some of the wealthiest minds to ever live you will uncover a hidden truth. The truth is that are brains emulate a radio. We receive and send out signals from our brain. Those signals are thoughts. Thoughts hold immense power, why do you think writers do it for hours?

Remove Polar Opposites

There is always a reason, even if it takes many seasons. Time is not real, but constant. Your perception means everything, now it is up to you to expand your dreams. Time invested in self always comes with great reward. If wants are sacrificed for growth, the highest power reacts. Life is all about causation. There is a cause and effect to every decision.

Have you ever tried to eliminate good and bad? When you put in time, it is inevitable that your mind will consume the task at hand. The secret that many people miss is the power of *Imagination*, chapter 6. What if I told you that entering the future was real?

The more sacrifices that you make for this universe to operate in harmony, the more sacrifices the universe will make for you. Do you want the key to accomplishing your dreams? The key is to not chase the material because it is merely controlled by the invisible. When you operate out of desire, passion and love will radiate from you, creating a magnetic aura.

Many people know of *The Secret*. *The Secret* is a popular book, explaining a concept called attraction. Many don't know of the source that it was originated from. I discovered the source, in a book written centuries ago. Attraction is only one component of the entire equation. In chapter nine, *Manifestation*, I will teach you how to complete the equation and how it transformed my life.

Finding Purpose

What is the purpose of life? The purpose of life is to gravitate towards love and away from fear. Love transforms you internally, which recreates you externally. Instead of chasing things, when operating out of love, things begin to gravitate towards you. We all want things overnight, but there are many hidden secrets to this life.

Greatness is not something that you can create overnight. At one point frustration ruled over me because I wanted my dreams instantly. The generation we live in today is heavily influenced by social media. We all want millions overnight because we see it on social media. The easy access to social media has affected our psychology as a society.

Illusion of Social Media

What makes social media so dangerous is that our ability to see things instantly, makes us feel as though we should be able to achieve it just as quickly. Social media has created an influx in grandiosity. This new style of communication makes it easy to create a false image. Our presence becomes limitless because of the accessibility to anyone in the world, at any moment in time.

As someone scrolls through social media, mirror neurons fire, which spring emotions to the surface. Mirror neurons are important to understand. As a human it is important to know that watching someone do something activates the same neurons as performing the same action. Being able to see someone instantly creates a feeling of openness, creating a feeling as if you know them.

Social media also gives people the ability to turn their real life into a virtual type of world. People use social media to create false images all the time and at many moments it has fooled millions of people. The power of social media has made people think that success comes overnight. Less emphasis has been place on the process. More emphasis has been placed on the easy schemes and shortcuts to achieve things.

Avoid the Moment

Have you ever taken the time to stop and think? Those who fall a victim to the current moment always get left behind. Would you like another key? You must learn how to become a forward thinker. Those who reach great heights are oftentimes visionaries. Visionaries know how to dissect images, allowing sight into the bigger picture.

I lived my dreams long before I walked in them. Now that I am here it is easy to navigate. My message is beginning to polarize the audience who will benefit most. By the time you reach these words it will be my past, but your present. Are you following along?

Never fall too deep into the moment. While you must live in the moment, know that your thoughts must be focused on the future. Your current situation is a result of past thoughts. I never wanted to be average. Many people are existing, not living, what are you doing?

The mind of the great differs from the mind of the average. If greatness is the goal, thoughts, at all times, must be under control. *The Ancient Key* is designed to unlock your mind. When the mind is unlocked it is easier to create with the imagination and manifest a vision, through action.

Become a Magnet

Once you understand how to control the emotions you radiate with, you will emulate a magnet. The energy you put out, influences the people and experiences that enters your life. Love is the highest energy and has the ability to resonate with everybody around you, even people you've never met or who is not yet alive.

Life is unpredictably amazing. It only takes one day for your life to change. Three months ago, I was a college student trying to figure out if this plan would manifest. I just wanted my professors to pass me on all the test so I wouldn't have to deal with any stress. What if I told you I was blessed and so are you?

The day I graduated, I launched my business. A week later, I published *First in the Family*. A week after that I sold out of the first volume, which was all signed, with a written note. 50 people from around the world believed in me enough to buy one of my first 50 copies, which transformed into inspiration for me.

My Unbroken Promise

I made a promise that I would become one of the greatest and each book would be worth over $1,000,000. The thing about prosperity is that it comes with peace, wealth and chosen destiny. When you help someone else up the ladder their life will always be connected to yours. I am giving back everything that I can, before the world finds me and I am no longer as available as I once was.

Time is not real. In other words, my first 50 books are already worth millions. It's just in a different time period. Building wealth is not just about self, it's about everyone but yourself, everyone around you and after you. When the light shines through you, you have ability to cast it on others. When you shine the light it creates more opportunities.

Wealth is very powerful because it goes beyond your lifetime. Other generations benefit from the sacrifices that you make today, the law of causation, which can lead to great manifestations. If you make sacrifices today, you can help someone that isn't alive yet. If I were to die today, these words, they are still going to live. My mind is now forever in the ether, chapter 8, *Mastermind*, meaning people will always be able to connect with me.

Master the Science

When you understand the universe, life becomes easy. Life is all about perceptions. People will try to argue with you about what is wrong and right, but there is no such thing. I don't argue with people because I have conducted my own research, constructing my own truth and that is what I suggest you do too.

People are often sucked into things because of the influence around them. When you self-educate you discover hidden information, which will allow you to develop your own truth. Create your own reality and live out every dream you ever imagined. Few will believe in you, until you get the material.

People in society always gravitate towards things that are physical. If it's physical, then they crave. If it's physical, then they believe, but as long as you have something in your mind, then most will always be weary. I've had this book written for many years. I've told people about this book and my plan to inspire millions for many years, but it was hard for some because of their constant fear within, about their own lives.

There is something in this life called projection. People project their feelings onto the world, which drastically affects their reality. Some people have been through failures and setbacks, which creates fear to chase any other dream. What this does is project a light that is shined on other people. Instead of seeing the possibilities in the other person's life, they project their emotions, causing lack of belief.

Set Your Limits

Some people, they laughed at me. Some people, they told me I would never make it. How should you deal with doubt? I transformed the energy into a positive force. What is the key to self-love?

The key is to never let anyone dictate your limits. When you take control of your own life, by using your thoughts to reprogram your mind, which we will talk about, you understand that life is really in your hands. *The Ancient Key* is the blueprint that I have built for myself. Many people are wondering how I am growing so rapidly. They are questioning if it's fabricated, so what's the best way to show someone?

Instead of speaking about what I plan to do, I am acting on my original plan. Are you taking action on your original plan? Our thoughts are the seeds, meaning that is yet, another key. When you unlock your mind, the invisible becomes visible, giving you control, which connects you directly to your soul.

"The moment you take action, the concealed is revealed, which can create chills."

-**Ken Viñales**

2

Concealed

Be Aware

The information that you are going to receive may be hard to believe. In the beginning it was hard for me. What is most important goes far beyond what you can physically see. What do I mean? This world that we are living in, consists of other worlds that is invisible to the naked eye. Our five senses limits us.

They don't teach you about this. Who is they? They are your teachers. They are your parents. They are your friends. They are the media. They can be yourself.

One day I began asking myself questions. That small action forced me to looked outside of my reality. Shortly after, various perspectives that were previously unavailable began to appear.

We spend so many years in a school system. Many years of our life consists of receiving education from an outside source. How many people educate themselves outside of the school system? It took me 17 years to read a book on my own time, without anyone instructing me to do so.

We are raised in households. In our household we learn morals, communication and develop an attachment style. Outside of our household, we spend many years inside of a institution that educates us, based on their curriculum. Have you ever asked yourself who makes the curriculum?

The reason self-education is important is because it gives you power. The power comes because you choose what you want to learn about. Those who understand the concept of consistency reap the benefits of polarized energy. School taught me useless subjects that came with no benefit. Self-education taught me to direct my focus on one subject because focus is energy and more energy equals power.

The power that comes from directed energy is something called Mastery. Whatever your mind is exposed to it conforms to. What makes what our parents teach us the right way? Have you ever lived in a different country? Why are people's beliefs different?

The best thing that you can start doing is asking questions. Always ask why. Why are you who you are? Why do you believe in what you believe in? Why do you love the way you love? When I began asking myself deeper questions about the world, society and psychology I was forced out of my comfort zone.

Why do they force us to take irrelevant subjects in school? Could it be a distraction? Have you ever wondered when the shift in society is going to happen? Why should I spend years learning things such as algebra, chemistry and history if it will not help me succeed in my actual reality?

Questions are Key

When you ask yourself uncomfortable questions it causes you to think outside the box. When outside the box two things can happen. Fear can emerge, causing you to go back inside the box or faith can takeover. Faith has led to some of the world's greatest discoveries.

Take a moment to think about how much technology has revolutionized over the past decade. Every year there is something new. Every year there is a new version of some electronic, car or company, but think about this. In the past two or more centuries, our school system has operated under the same principles and curriculum. For many years I thought that I was a failure in school, but that is far from the truth.

The school system fails those who want to be entrepreneurs. The school system fails those who desire financial freedom. When I first discovered *The Ancient Key*, it was hard for me to digest. Why? How can you believe in something that you cannot physically see? Overtime that is when my mind began to realize. The invisible is what creates the material.

Financial freedom does not come when you work for money. Happiness doesn't come when you are a slave to a corporation. You must learn to make money in your sleep to officially become free. Many feel as though striving for material goals is the way to go. The answer is always going to be no.

If the invisible creates the material and you chase the material, the invisible is controlling you. What is the invisible? Our emotions are invisible to us, but they can be influenced by outside sources. Material things create short term feelings of satisfaction that eventually go away with time.

In order to take advantage of *The Ancient Key*, you must learn to see yourself outside of yourself. When you unlock multiple perspectives it gives you limitless potential. Most of this information is concealed. It's in old books. It's in old research. It's not taught or promoted.

Isolation from World

Many people wish for wealth, but don't know the first step. Self-education is the first step. Taking this step will open the door to mental, spiritual and financial freedom. When I discovered this information, I was unaware that it would lead me on this journey. My only option became to walk with faith. I took one step at a time.

For three hours per day I spent time writing in my bedroom. Three hours per day, engaged in any task will equivalate to one thousand hours per year. Ten thousand hours equals Mastery. What was I trying to master? I began by reading books, years later it transformed into me writing books.

Initially my desire came from wanting to get rich. Social media has made us desire becoming rich overnight. Humans now have direct access to people's lives, which can create desires. These desires are so strong that people begin acting out to draw attention to themselves, which only creates dissonance in the mind.

When I embarked on this journey, part of me thought success would come overnight. It took two years of consistency to comprehend how the universe operates. Many wish for wealth. Many wish for their dream life. Few make the necessary sacrifices.

There are no secrets only years of confusion, sacrifices and mistakes. When you put in the time, the stars will align. This information is easy to find. This information is not promoted. How do you go to the next level?

Instead of implanting useless information in your mind, take control. The more you search, the more perspectives you will have. I wanted to research the source. My desire transformed to acquiring wisdom from centuries ago.

Much of my life has been spent in a school system. Many of my years consisted of studying information that hasn't helped me accomplish any of my dreams. In other words, the school system has failed me. The common mistake that most people make is that they never educate themselves outside of school.

To Learn is to Earn

We are not taught how to educate ourselves because so many of our years are spent taking orders. We develop the trait to obey. When is the last time you've read a personal development book? Do you invest thousands of hours into your craft? Have you ever tried to teach yourself a new skill?

Learning is not boring, it is rewarding. At one point in time I hated reading. I walked away from writing, but that is only because of the association that I made with school. Self-education gives you power over your mind.

Do you spend hours per day on your vision? How much time have you read outside of the institution that you were condition in? When is the last time you wrote a descriptive version of your future life in words? What if you were a few steps away from entering your dream?

Break away from what you were exposed to. Learn to look at yourself from multiple angles. It is important to look outside of schooling and parents for information. What we are exposed to is neither right nor wrong. There is just more to this world and universe. If you want to discover who you are at the root, expanding your mind is necessary.

If you never take a look outside of your own reality, then you will forever be mentally trapped. The inability to expand your perspective will lead to many illusions, which can cause failure. Failure is one of the greatest things that a human can experience. More wisdom can be obtained from failure than success.

In my moments of failure, growth came about. Great individuals understand there is more to learn from failures than successes. A failed goal can change an individual's perception of reality. When you reflect on who you are, your self-awareness will increase. A high self-awareness allows for supreme control.

Limitation of Environment

If you are born into something it is hard to see outside of that because of conformity. The key to growth is stepping outside of that because it will test your comfort zone. I am not suggesting that you change your beliefs or morals, but just be open to gaining new insights on information, that you did not have before. My life didn't change until I started to realize that there is more to life than what I was previously aware of. A spiritual awakening happened when I was 17 years old.

At 17 years old we are searching for ourselves. We are trying to figure out the best route to take for our future and it can be extremely difficult trying to decide. That is what led me to isolating myself. That is when I began studying the universe. In the beginning it created shock.

Shock can happen due to a sudden surprise. These concepts are not taught in school or by our parents so reading about this information created shock. I was finding books that were written in different centuries. That is when I began to learn about the world of energy, frequencies and ether. *The Ancient Key* is a universal blueprint that will translate to any time period, gift or vision.

The original application of these different concepts did not result in what I initially expected. My mind had to be reprogrammed. I was used to living my life a certain way. My perception of the world was biased based on my preconceived beliefs. I was forced to see the world for what it actually is, not for what I thought it was.

Greatness is in You

Every human has greatness within. Whether you believe it or not, you are one of the greatest humans to ever walk this earth. You must believe in you before anyone else. No one else is going to believe in you, unless you believe in you. We are all made up of the same atoms, molecules and electrons. In other words, the greatness a legend has within is the same greatness you have within.

Remove every limitation from your mind. Information will be easier to find. When were you ever taught that thoughts were things? Did you know that there are worlds, inside of this world? We only have five senses, so it is impossible to sense things such as vibrations and frequencies, but they do exist.

We are taught algebra and geometry, but why aren't we taught how to research? We are rarely given the correct information to become the individuals that we desire to be. Knowledge is important for accomplishing large goals. The most difficult thing is learning what steps need to be taken when first beginning.

Practical Success Methods

If you aren't given a formula how will you ever learn?
At one point in time I was confused. My mother is an entrepreneur, so I always had access to a business owner. Another key is knowing how to use your resources. There are people that you have access to that could provide you with important information, have you had that conversation yet? My mother owned her business for 30 years, but never went to school, which made me realize that school wasn't the determining factor.

My mother, in fact, struggled in school. Outside of school she never educated herself either, she just learned through experiences. For that reason she never was able to teach me the science of the universe, society and thoughts. Learning psychology helped unlock my mind, giving me access to perspectives that are supernatural.

There is a science to greatness and success, but it took me years to find the blueprint. It was naturally embedded in me because of my mother. I am the next generation, which means it is up to me to take her greatness to another level. What if I told you it was possible to transform your reality? That is the magic of *The Ancient Key*.

From a young age the media has brainwashed us to believe that greatness is a matter of luck. We are conditioned to believe that we are either born with it or without it. Some people live their life with that belief. If you live your life believing in luck, events will happen randomly. Have you ever been tired of not having control over your own life?

Why should there be an age limit on dreams? I am showing people that they can live their dreams if they take directed leaps of faith. When I began this journey, I didn't understand what was going to happen. I didn't understand how I would connect with people. How do you reach more people if your platform is small? The journey to your dreams will be an emotional uphill battle, but never lose faith. Never not self-educate.

Don't Live Blind

Many concepts exist that goes beyond our conscious awareness. If you never take the time to search for what you don't know, then you will never learn new things. Have you tried explaining colors to someone that can't see? Can you explain the beauty of music to someone that can't hear? In other words, expose your mind to as many new perspectives and experiences as possible.

Being closed minded comes with many drawbacks. Those who never expose themselves to things that go against what they were taught creates an unconscious bias for themselves. If you close off your mind, you're only hurting yourself. When I began to take a look outside of myself, from outside of myself, that's when I began to see that many people in society are just robots.

Many humans wake up, go to work, eat, sleep and repeat. The older we get the further we get pulled into other people's dreams and away from ours. For so many years many humans live their life as another number.

There are existing rather than living. Once I realized that I did not want to become another number in society, my awakening occurred, breaking me free from the chains that were wrapped around my mind.

No matter how much you think you are living in truth, no one technically knows how humans came to be. No one knows what this world really is. The truth is whatever you believe the truth to be. How do you find truth? You find truth by research and experimentation.

Discover Your Truth

The best way to get in tune with yourself is to begin educating yourself. Don't fall victim to the system. Don't fall victim to what your parents teach. Don't fall victim to what you believe. You need to learn how to expand your mind by going back in time.

At 22 years old, I sold my first book and it made it to nine different countries. That suggested that I was given a power to inspire and transform lives. People who now see or meet me, feel a connection and want to better themselves. They want to reach their highest potential and as a human, if you're not trying to grow yourself, then you are subconsciously hurting yourself. The goal is to learn how to connect your soul, mind, and body. That is the quickest way to reach harmony.

Harmony is the universal goal. Harmony is the way that you reach your full potential and once you reach your full potential you will be able to accomplish every single goal that you set for yourself. Life is about building your wealth. Wealth is about generating a profit and prosperity in other individuals' lives. The key is the better each succeeding generation.

Illusion of Material

A lot of people, they strive for material things, but why strive for material things? When you can make material things strive for you. I am not an individual who strives for material things, but instead I create a force that causes the material to gravitate towards me. The way to do that is by realizing that what's inside of you has more control than what is outside of you. Once you are in tune with yourself than everything around you will gravitate towards you, forming the reality that you desire.

Everything physical first began in the mind. When you use your imagination to construct a vision, it has no choice but to manifest with directed action. The concealed is what you haven't been taught. Nothing that you have been taught is the full truth. The way that you find truth is to seek truth and once you begin to seek truth, you will begin to place yourself in positions that will reveal truth to you, but you cannot run from it.

Truth is going to be difficult to digest because it is going to go against every single thing that you have been taught in your life. It may go against your religion and it may go against your beliefs. It may go against some of the things that you have built your whole entire reality upon, but that is when an awakening occurs. You have so much control over your own life and over your own future. The only thing holding you back is learning how to gain that control.

Once you gain control, you are able to resonate with and wake up other souls. Sometimes you may have to spend hours alone so that your mind can clear itself from the outside influences. When you detach yourself from society and other people it allows you to reprogram your mind. It will be difficult at first, but that is the key to finding out who you are inside.

Once you find out who you are inside, you are able to connect with your purpose. The concealed is now revealed. The power to change your life is in your ability to enhance your mind. Take the time and I promise the stars will align so you no longer have to live blind.

"Logic blinds, instincts awaken, set a direct destination and your mind will find a way to make it."

-**Ken Viñales**

3

Blind Control

How it Seemed

Before *Think and Grow Rich* by Napoleon Hill entered my life, my mindset on life was not optimistic. To my knowledge, people were either gifted, cursed or regular. I thought that greatness was a matter of luck, not consistency and patience. Books entered my life at the perfect time, which eventually helped me find my why.

Have you ever wondered why some people are great? What if it was possible to acquire the skillset of some of the greatest men to ever live? So many people live life thinking that supreme skills are inborn, but that is the furthest thing from the truth. What if I told you the way to gain control, was by giving up control?

The reason why reading is essential to your success is because of the knowledge you are able to acquire. Books expand your internal world, by revealing to you information that was once unavailable. I have never liked reading, but there is something about knowledge that excites me. The reason why people are being changed by my books is because my words are for the non-readers.

Find the Truth

People who do not like to read, love my work. The reason stems from my ability to see life from various perspectives. At 17 years old, I was just an innocent teen, trying to get rich by any means. There were times where I contemplated doing illegal things for money. Then one day I stumbled upon something that would change my entire mindset about the world around us.

What if I told you that the truth has been concealed from you? What if I told you that you can do whatever you put your mind to? This concept is often misinterpreted because of the simplicity, but there is a science behind what I am teaching. This chapter is going to take you on a mental journey, leading you directly to your soul, which will give you a precise destination to go.

What is blind control? Thinking outside the box is all that I have come to know. What I am going to reveal to you is something that may have never crossed your mind. For 17 years, I was unaware of this hidden power within me. Did you know this power is within you? Many people are living unwanted lives so allow me to tell you why.

Mistaken Awakening

When I was 17, I discovered something about the human mind and universe that you must know. You need to know this information in order to get to where you want to go. Humans are so caught up and things that are right in front of them. Many don't take the time to realize how powerful the present moment is. The material is created by the invisible, which means everything around you, even this book all began in the mind.

When I first began college my mind was focused on money. *How can I make millions? What job will provide me with a six figure salary? What degree would make me the most money?* These are questions that haunted me daily. As a college student it's stressful thinking about the future because the uncertainty of what will happen next creates and instill fear.

The shift for me happened when I started searching through the unseen. The first key to reaching a higher level of thinking is understanding your brain. Once you unlock your mind, it will open up doors that were once locked. In society many individuals are unaware of who they are internally, which makes it hard for them to understand other's.

Ignore all Doubters

There was much confusion in the people around me, when I chose the psychology route. No one understood the effect of mind power. We all have greatness bestowed in us the day we come to life, which made me realize this path is right. What often goes unnoticed is that although we have one brain, we have two minds within. Would you like to know more?

My information about the mind is not easy to find. The reason that my words hold much weight is because I have lived everything that I am speaking to you about. The problem with the world is that it is being run by leaders who do not practice what they preach. When I first discovered psychology, I had no clue that it would not only awaken me, but also those around me.

How much time have you spent studying yourself? The crazy thing about life is that we, humans, spend countless hours studying random subjects. Subjects that cannot be applied in the real world, but very few spend time tracking thoughts and habits. It is easy to feel like you are in control, but many people are mentally enslaved.

Why do you think 10 percent of the world controls 90 percent of the income? What if I told you that you are not free? What if I told you that our encounter was meant to be? There is much information out there, but it can sometimes be hard to find, especially information about the subconscious and conscious mind. Upon entering college I had no clue what the difference or purpose of each were. Now, today, after five years of research and application it has become obvious why there is so much power in understanding what is being shared with you.

Search for Truth

What often goes unnoticed is the importance of self-education. From ages 4 to 18 we are required to go to school. In school we are taught about a wide variety of subjects, but how many classes have you taken that have introduced you to these different concepts? When you begin to educate yourself, it is a unique way of building your wealth. With knowledge comes power, with power comes opportunities and that leads unity of mind, body and soul. Are you wondering what makes your mind so special?

The conscious mind is what you are using to read these words. The conscious mind is also the mind that allows you to concentrate on certain tasks. What you must realize, right now, today, is the mind you are using to focus is blinding you. What do I mean by this? Are you wondering how you have gone so many years, unaware of this fact?

We, humans, are the only species who have the ability to make a decision. At one point in time, we were purely instinctual, but overtime we developed consciousness and with that comes confusion. Have you ever thought about the limitations that comes with living in this world? Allow me to break this down.

When we enter this world we are only allowed five senses. Those who are wise unlock the sixth sense. Are you aware of your sixth sense yet? The handicap to only having five senses is that there are things happening around us and in this universe that cannot be detected. A perfect example is vibrations and frequencies.

The Hidden Realm

Don't you see? Whenever you speak, vibrations are being released. This is an undeniable fact. All you have to do is record your voice and you can see the different frequencies depending on your tone and pitch. Like most 17 year old teenagers, it was hard for me to understand the universe. For some people they die, before ever realizing there is an invisible world that cannot be detected, but only sensed.

School or parents do not teach this information. How can you be aware of something that you are not exposed to? In other words, we will always be blind to what we cannot see. I found out who I am and where I evolved from through self-education, research and experimentation. Not many people understood my direction, but from the very beginning I could see the reflection, the reflection of the future me, the future me that is now speaking directly to you.

I acquired a B.A. in Psychology because it would give me a scientific foundation of the mind. The mind is what creates everything around us. How much time have you spent studying the conscious and the subconscious? This chapter is going to outline why it is important that you remove all limitations from your mind. What you must realize is that as a human, even with eyes, you are blind.

Foundation of Universe

This universe consists of atoms, molecules, and electrons. Have you ever seen an electron with your eyes? No, but they're around you. They are a part of you. They are within you. Are you aware of what this means? This suggest that there is another world around us, which we are blind too.

Now that you have an understanding of the invisible world, let's go deeper. Why are you who you are today. Millions of years ago, humans were subconscious animals, that means we lived off instinct. We didn't have the free-will to make a decision. We couldn't consciously choose, but one day consciousness took over and that is how it all began.

Consciousness gives us the power to choose. Through this consciousness we have the option to freely make a decision, which makes people think they have control. The development of consciousness led to other things, such as right and wrong, good and bad, devil and God.

When you think about life from an evolutionary perspective, it forces you to think outside the box. *What is real? What is right? Who am I? Where did I come from?* Every day questions like those began to enter my mind.

Development of Consciousness

Take a step back. Go all the way to the beginning of time. What if I told you that in the past there are many treasures that can unlock your mind? If humans were not always conscious, then how did we live? The first step to unlocking your true power is understanding the instinctual nature that is forever embedded within you.

The subconscious mind is what is the ruler. The subconscious mind is what is truly controlling you. That is blind control. It may seem like your decisions are in your control, but little do you know that is not how it goes. The present time is determined by what was allowed in your subconscious mind.

Now, how do you apply this in your regular life? When I began to study the mind, I didn't understand what exactly I would find, but overtime the stars have aligned. Have you discovered who you are on the inside? I am an individual who operates out of love, my goal is to make an impact on the world, something many people dream to do. What makes me different?

The Separation Factor

If you are reading this, then you too have a goal to do big things. What if I told you that it was possible to manifest big dreams? Early in my journey it was hard to imagine myself inspiring millions, but now I am here inspiring, not only you, but millions of other's in time periods that have not been physically lived by me.

How do you make a change on the world when there are billions of other people? How do you make a change when there are millions of other ideas? How can you make an entrance into the world, shocking everyone that you come in contact with? These are questions that you must ask yourself. These are questions that are designed to increase your overall wealth.

When I began writing something sparked within me, forcing me to time travel, using my thoughts. In other words, when you enter past experiences, new information that was once not available will be revealed. What this will do is allow you to see why you are the person you are today. The person I am today originated from the experiences and encounters that I attracted, chapter 7, at a young age.

I never knew that I would end up here, talking to you, in this position because as a young adolescent, I was blind. The more I embraced my ability to write, the more free my mind became. Did you know that it is possible to use your conscious mind to program your subconscious mind? This concept is difficult to understand because of the amount of time it takes to manifest, chapter 9, things into the physical world.

Behind the Scenes

Allow me to explain exactly what your subconscious mind is and why it is imperative that you understand how to control it. The mind that pumps your heart, keeps your lungs going and scans the environment is your subconscious. You are not consciously doing those things, it is an automatic process that keeps you alive. In other words, even when you are not aware, the subconscious mind is always working to keep you alive and safe.

As I mentioned, humans have not always had the ability to choose. We lived off of instincts and evolved into what we are today. What often goes unnoticed is how to take advantage of this fact. The only mind that knows right and wrong is the conscious. The subconscious does not know what right or wrong is, it only knows to act.

How can this be used to your advantage? With your conscious mind you have the ability to think. With thoughts you can purposely implant, in your subconscious mind, desires, goals and dreams. When you do this your subconscious will not know right from wrong because it only knows to act. The day I found out this truth my life changed forever.

Greatest Book Ever

During my freshman year of college *Think and Grow Rich* introduced me to this magical power. At first I was skeptical. It was not something that I was taught. It was not something that people around me were speaking about, but something told me that it was real so my only option was to implement the formulas and strategies that the author, Napoleon Hill provided.

The first thing I began doing was writing down exactly what I wanted. Have you ever considered that your current is your past? Did you know your future is your current? The first step to taking control of your subconscious is by giving it a specific direction. My life up until college was ruled by failure because of my inability to direct my mind.

I did not understand that the mind could be studied. I was not aware that indecisiveness was the quickest route to failure. College was a wakeup call for me because it made me realize that there was no more time to waste, which is why I began to go back in time, using my thoughts. *Think and Grow Rich* was written in the 1900's, but I have recreated the methods and formulas in today's generation and this encounter is an example of manifestation.

The Power of Words

What I have realized is that few people have control over their life. The sad part is that many are afraid to take control because of the pressure that comes with it. Many people want to know how to unlock the subconscious mind power, but few take the time to search for the information they need. The first step to entering the subconscious is by using your words to provide a specific direction.

What does this mean? Words can be used as affirmations. Affirmations have been studied for many years and there is a science to their effectiveness. Affirmations work because you implant beliefs into your subconscious mind. Once a belief is affirmed through writing or speech, that command enters your subconscious, it accepts it and you will unconsciously act out in ways that confirms those beliefs.

When I discovered my purpose, I told myself that *I am going to be the greatest*. At that time, I was not sure what would lead to me going down in history. I just knew overtime, situations would lead to me doing things that would put me in the conversation with some of the greatest humans to ever live.

Remove Mental Limitations

The hard part about a journey is loving the process. In this new generation, especially being a millennial it is easy to fall into traps, wanting things to happen overnight. The problem is that it takes countless hours, sacrifices and perfect timing for great ideas to materialize. If you take control of your mind by embedding certain commands and affirmations, you can become as great as you want to be. The only limitations are those that exist in your mind, just have faith and remember there is no such thing as time.

When I began to understand the subconscious mind, I took a break away from everything. I stopped watching TV. I stopped using social media. I stopped hanging around people. I stopped partying. I became reserved, closing myself off from the world.

It may sound crazy to some, but when you want to reprogram your mind any outside influence can deter the process. The reason that I chose to cut off the world is because without sacrifice there will not be growth. The subconscious mind is always at work, absorbing everything that it is exposed too. That was the first step I took to taking control of my future.

It is impossible to isolate yourself from the world. That is not the point trying to be communicated. You must understand that when you are engaged in a task your subconscious mind is working, taking in things that you cannot process consciously. What this means is that you may think you are making the decision in the present time, but that decision was already predetermined by what was allowed in your subconscious mind.

You Are Brainwashed

Big name brand companies and organizations, brainwash society by using the media, creating something known in psychology as the mere exposure effect. When you are exposed to a certain idea, image or brand it literally becomes a part of who you are, whether you want it to or not. The more you see something, the more likely it will cause you to analyze and think about it.

When I began to take time away from people and the media, there was a shift in my perception. It was as if my mind began to cleanse itself, ridding all the negativity, doubts and fear. I slowly began to understand what was really going on in, not only my life, but yours as well. What if I told you that we are all being brainwashed, far beyond our awareness?

When I removed the world, from my world, it minimized the outside influence of ideas, thoughts and images of other people. Are you wondering how to capitalize off of blind control? We are programmed. Programming is another way to say brainwashed. The key to this theory is using your words and thoughts to direct your subconscious mind in the direction that you want, removing the influence of society or the media.

Determine Your Fate

What fails to be addressed is that there is no such thing as true or false, only cause and effect. Reality is false, dreams are real. Your subconscious mind is what creates your outside reality. The key to living out your dreams is to brainwash yourself with your own beliefs. Do not let the outside world dictate how great you can be.

At 19 years old, the spirit awakened in me. I removed the limitations from my mind and began to see that everything was going to manifest, with action, in due time. If you believe that you are great, you are going to attract experiences, that create situations, leading you to become great. If you don't believe that you can achieve something, your subconscious mind is going to create an outside reality that does not lead you to achieving that goal. The power is not in what you can consciously do, but what you can consciously implant in your subconscious mind to do.

Growing up, I didn't know what would happen in my life. For nearly 12 years I wished for an athletic scholarship, but did not put in the correct amount of hours. Not only that I allowed doubt to enter my mind, which created an outside reality of failure. Why should people believe in you if you don't believe in yourself?

For many years, I didn't have real confidence. I only acted like I had confidence on the outside, but with the subconscious mind it doesn't matter about surface level. People can sense doubt. People can sense fear. People didn't respect me because I didn't respect myself.

The Missing Piece

Self-education is the key to tapping into your internal power. The subconscious mind is the control panel. Humans evolved to consciousness in three different stages. We went from purely instincts, to gaining consciousness and for the elite they become conscious of their consciousness.

What I learned about the mind, it forced me to shift my energy. I wanted to take control and the only way to do that is by learning how to properly use your two minds. You must use your conscious mind to reprogram your subconscious mind. The conscious mind is a director. The subconscious is an order taker.

Your conscious mind can direct energy. What this means is that you can take an idea, vision or plan, and embed it into your nervous system so it has no choice but to manifest into the outside world. Many people buy self-help books, but few are actually able to incorporate this theory into a story that shows how and why it works with exact experiences.

The way I gained power was through writing. Have you ever tried to write out your future? I took years to write out exactly who and what I wanted to be. What that did was recreate my reality and put me in positions that would lead to that goal materializing in the real world. Now it is many years later and you are here, absorbing this life changing formula.

No Overnight Success

I am not here today because something happened overnight. I am here today because I read, prayed, reprogramed my mind and life changed, day by day, overnight. What you need to understand is that once you give your subconscious mind all of the control, then you will know that any goal is going to be achievable. Why that happens is because your subconscious mind doesn't know right from wrong, it only knows to go.

College changed me because I saw that 99 percent of students didn't know where or who they wanted to be. People were going back and forth. They didn't know what major to choose. They weren't sure if they wanted a job, to own a business or go back to school. A life changing day for me came when I defined my destination.

When you define exactly what you want in your mind, then it will happen, as long as you follow up with consistent action. You may think you are in control but no. Your subconscious mind is in control and if you aren't taking control of your thoughts, then your thoughts are taking control of your subconscious and your subconscious is taking control of your life.

Reprogram the Mind

If you understand that you don't have control over much, but your thoughts you will enter a different realm. *How do I find my purpose? How do I control my thoughts?* These were my thoughts before rediscovering my gift. The simplest and easiest way to do so is by writing and by reading.

Reading and writing enhances your concentration. Concentration allows you to focus your thoughts for longer periods of time. When you are able to focus your thoughts for longer periods of time, you are able to build up more energy. When you are able to build up more energy you are able to attract things to you, which we will talk about in chapter 5, *Radiation*.

See life is a science. Success can be broken down into multiple equations. When you combine these different strategies together, that is how you create *The Ancient Key*, which you will one day need. You can accomplish all of your goals and dreams, but first you must believe!

"This universe you live in, also lives in you, but you must, first search for the truth."

-Ken Viñales

4

You-niverse

Unknown Perspective

Life is all about perspectives. That is why there is no such thing as right and wrong. The only thing that exists is cause and effect. There is a consequence to every action, whether it is positive or negative. The moment I began researching the deeper meanings of life, the consequence was discoveries.

What if I told you that you are nothing more than a universe, inside of the universe, experiencing the universe? When I was introduced to that perspective an immediate power came over me. Is that what they mean when they say greatness is inside of everyone? Now, please be aware. This information I am sharing with you is going to be hard to grasp because it is not often talked about, especially in any of the institutions or environments that we are raised in.

Respect all Beliefs

My goal is not to change beliefs, but to empower individuals with thoughts. Thoughts provoke curiosity, which can lead to life changing revelations. Reading changed me at my roots because of the amount of reflection that it caused me to do. When I first began reading it was difficult to find good books, but as I invested more time, more books that related to my situation began to appear.

I once lived my life thinking I was powerless. I glorified celebrities and great individuals, but did not understand that I had the same capabilities as them. You must know who you are inside because that will allow you to come alive outside. The only way to live a fulfilling life is to discover your inner-gift, which will put you on a path to reaching your highest-self.

Powerful Wisdom Inside

I have spent many years studying our universe, psychology and success and although I'm not a master at all these fields, my understanding is transcendent. A wise individual knows that they do not know much. I will never claim to be a master of this world that we live in, but I am confident in the wisdom that I have created and the knowledge that I have gained. This unique understanding of the world has allowed me to begin a path to greatness.

What I want to do for people is provoke thoughts. My goal is not to change beliefs, but to help build dream realities. I am promoting that people should do their own research because that is how you develop truth. My process is nowhere near over, but I've learned many things today that I didn't know before. New thoughts have found their way to me. To me, *The Ancient Key* is necessary to unlock hidden doors that are invisible to you.

If you desire a fruitful and prosperous life, this should not be your only source of wisdom. What you must take from this book is that self-education is the first step to greatness. What I mean by you are the universe, inside the universe, experiencing the universe, is that humans have a power that goes far beyond what we are taught in any school system, at home and or exposed to by the media. We are all connected to a higher source. In other words, we are all one with the universe. You are a human, but there is more to you than you know.

The Community Within

When you look into the mirror, what you are seeing is not a single entity, but a community. We live in a society that is within a society that is within another society. Societies make up our world, but our world is within another system that is within more systems. Now what does this mean? What this means is that the human body is made up of trillions of different cells so you, yourself, are not a single body, but a collection of different living organisms that have their own purpose.

You do not need to be an expert in biology to know that we are made up of cells. We were taught this in school at a young age. What we aren't taught is that these cells are just as alive as we are, with their own purpose and systems. So looking into the mirror is not a reflection of a single entity, but a community, a society. Just like the real world, there is a governor over this community and that is your mind.

The human mind governs each single cell that makes up the community, which is our human body. You can make that analogy to the universe itself. We are just cells inside of a large universe, with our own purpose, but still connected, which is why harmony must be perfected. We are the universe inside of the universe.

Universal Similarities

The universe itself, is a system that is made up of smaller systems. This is an undeniable fact. The reason that I say we are the universe experiencing the universe is because we are all made up of the same exact things. You are made up of cells, just like I am made up of cells. We are surrounded by atoms, molecules and electrons just like everyone else.

When you accept this fact it will allow you to unlock the greatness that is inside of you. That is why I believe in every person that I meet because at the root they are just like me. I believe in you, although I may never meet you because there is greatness in you, just like there is greatness in every other legend that has walked our earth.

You must use your mind, the governor, to direct your future. Like a governor directs and controls societies that is what your mind does for your body and soul. If you are directing your cells with negative energy then, negativity will radiate throughout your body and attract that into your life. That is why you must invest your time into love because love always beats hate. Love is the answer to negativity, sending your life into a harmonious flow.

The universal goal of the is harmony. How does this happen? When you are operating out of love, surrounding yourself around love, and doing what you love, not only are you operating through God's will, but you are in God, around God and vice versa. Every single cell in your body has a purpose. That is why you must implant greatness in yourself because your cells will take form.

Direct Your Mind

When I wake up every morning, I tell myself how great I am and what I want to be in life. I am not only giving the trillions of cells in my body a direct order and purpose, but also my subconscious mind and the universe. I am directing my mind to act out of love, which puts me in harmony with the infinite. The mind is so powerful that people have literally thought themselves into sickness do to improper thought control. Study your history and you will see, why thought is the beginning to everything that materializes into this world.

When you are stressing out, signals are being sent through your body, directing your cells to act in a negative way, which will produce various effects. If you do not learn how to think positive at all times it is a chance you are subconsciously harming yourself without even knowing it. On the flip side, there are people who have thought themselves out of sickness, by using their mind to direct their cells, leading them to a better health. I am not a biologist and will never claim to be, but it does not take much research to find this information and different cases. That is why self-education is so important.

All you need is the foundation to some of these different concepts and your life will transform. Do you want control or do you want to be lost and blind? We are all at different levels of consciousness in this world, living various truths, but we all have the ability to reach our full potential; it just takes time for the stars to align.

Cosmic Consciousness

Many people wonder what it takes to reach the highest level of consciousness, but it is not a hard concept. The easiest, yet most difficult way is to pray and or meditate. Through years of these practices you will connect with the infinite, providing you with a certain control of your thoughts that will prevent you from getting lost. Upon coming into this world, we don't have a choice. We come into consciousness and that's who we are.

We come into consciousness as this being, with a family and a story, in a certain environment. We do not choose that. The power comes because once we do come into this world, we are given a choice. The greats separate themselves from the average because of their ability to make good decisions. It first starts through building a vision. Great people read books. Great people are purposeful in their actions. Great people write down who they want to be long before they become it.

If you don't learn to take control of your thoughts, then you are not directing your community in the right direction. Are you comprehending?

You need to realize that your cells are alive as well. Your mind directs them. You are not just one single entity, but a community that is radiating with a vast amount of energy at different frequencies. Your thoughts are being sent out into the universe, which attracts energy, events and people back to you.

Greatness is Within

This universe we live in can be looked at as a television and each person has their own station. No station is greater than the other, but every single station is unique in their own way. We are all a part of this bigger system. A system that is impossible to consciously understand completely. When you realize that you have the same greatness as another legend, then it is apparent that life is only a matter of mindset.

You are the universe. The universe is you. You have greatness within you, but what often holds many of us back is the lack of belief. Once you begin to believe in yourself, then everyone else will gravitate towards you. Confidence is important for esoteric accomplishments. Be confident about your greatness and that will elevate you in unexplainable ways.

When I became conscious of my greatness, I began to move and operate in a certain way. At first it was hard embrace this level of consciousness with this level of confidence because insecure people fear those who are confident about their beliefs. Society tries to tear those down who believe in themselves.

Hate and Greatness

Once you accept that critics come with greatness then it will be easier to emerge into your greatness. The reason that I changed my beliefs and how I operate in society is because it doesn't matter how great you are or how awful you are, people will hate you just because you are great. That should not stop you from aligning yourself with God. God's will is going to lead you to a place called prosperity. Prosperity is important because it is the ultimate form of happiness. Not only are you going to find peace, but generate wealth and great health.

The key is to find other people who believe in themselves. Once you surround yourself around those who believe, it will rub off on you. When I began to walk on this spiritual journey, it led me to purpose because of the gift that awakened inside of me. I had to separate myself from many people because I didn't want outside influences affecting the frequency that I was trying to reach. This universe that we live in can be deduce down to energy and frequencies.

If you look in to the past, studying some of the world's greatest geniuses it will reveal the secrets to life. You are nothing more than energy. You are nothing more than the universe experiencing itself, through a certain level of consciousness. Once you realize who you are, the power that you have within will come alive. The power that you have within begins in your subconscious mind.

Study Your Thoughts

That is why you must find the time to study your life. You must use your words to implant exactly what you want into your subconscious. Your subconscious mind is going to create the reality that you desire. That is called power. It will take countless hours, but that is the sacrifice. That is how you change your life.

It took me to realize that I am the universe. It took me to embrace my power before my life changed. You are only moments away from connecting to your soul. Once you find your soul, you will be directed where to go, through the signs that you receive. Signs are being sent to you, daily. Those signs are your experiences, environment and people in your life.

Your life must be lived based off of faith. You must be willing to take the necessary steps to get to where you want to go. Devote all of your actions to fulfilling your purpose. That is the key. Once you realize that fact, you know that the most powerful thing in this universe is to act.

> "The human body emulates a magnet, causing people to gravitate or repel, out of an unconscious habit."
>
> -Ken Viñales

5

Radiation

Secret to Energy

The most underrated task in this world is concentration. What is concentration? Concentration is consciously focusing your attention on a certain task or idea, using your thoughts. If you want to succeed at a high level, then you need to enhance your ability to concentrate your thoughts for hours. The ability to concentrate for hours at a time builds the energy inside of and around you.

The world that we live in is made up of atoms and molecules, which can be deduced down to electrons. Electrons are invisible forms of energy that can influence the realm around you that cannot be seen only sensed. Once you accept this fact, you will understand the power of concentrating your forces, is the key to keeping your dreams intact.

All material things can be referred to as matter. Matter is just a combination of different electrons, protons, atoms and molecules, which means that nothing is technically solid. Look around you right now. Think about how solid this book feels in your hand. Now I want to shift your perspective and understanding of the universe. If you realize that everything around you is just an empty space and different forms of energy it will change your entire frequency.

Accept the Doubters

This information will not be accepted by everyone and that is okay. When I wrote this book I realized that my story would come with a variety of different opinions, but that did not stop me. Many people are living their life sleep, which is why I am here. My words are powerful enough to resonate with souls long after I am gone so that is why this must be done. The key to life is learning how to infuse your thoughts with high level emotions to create and find purpose.

When you live your life with purpose then your come to an understanding that your life is worth it. Directed thoughts change your energy and increase your frequency. How? All humans have an outside cloud around them that radiates and attracts. That cloud can be referred to as an aura. Whether you are conscious of this aura or not it can be sensed by other humans, dictating how they respond to your initial encounter.

The outside aura around you is what plays a part in the people, events and experiences that you attract in your life. What this means is that the world around you is determined by the amount of time you have spent concentrating on the life you want. What I once failed to realize is that most of my thinking was spent in the past or future. It was very rare for me to come into the present moment. How much time do you spend in the now? Think about it.

Initial Awakening

My initial awakening came when I met failure at 17. It was the day, when all of my fears were created. Thoughts create emotions and emotions influence actions. When you have thoughts that are infused with fear it causes you to act out in ways that lead to bad events. When you are living in fear it is hard to see that what you are feeling is not real, but just thoughts of things that have not occurred and may never occur.

My original dream in life was to become a professional basketball player. When I met failure it created thoughts of my future that were not pleasant. Do you know what it is like to dedicate over a decade of your life, only for the road to end abruptly? When my dream, was no longer in my reach it seemed like all the opportunities that I would eventually receive were seized. Failure can cause you to ruminate in the past, creating feelings of regret, which will influence negative actions in the current, dictating a future of continued failure.

Do you know what it is like to wish you were better? Have you ever looked in the mirror and hated the reflection? I spent months wishing about what I could have changed, but what does that change? Regret only causes you to go insane. My wakeup call came when I realized that the past is no longer. Your past has come and go. The only way to change is to connect with your soul.

Remove Fearful Thoughts

How do you align with your soul, when you don't know where to go? It begins with your mind. Your mind controls your thoughts. Your thoughts, when concentrated with purpose aligns not only the stars, but your body and mind with your soul. Many people, like myself at one point, meet failure continuously because of their consistency of negativity.

Fear has the ability to make you think about your future in a negative light. What many aren't aware of is that your current is created in your past and your future is created in your present. I was planting negative seeds in my own life, which created a negative aura around me. When your thoughts are negative it creates a false projection of reality, meaning that negative outcomes is all that you will see.

When you create images of failure that is what your energy is going to consist of, meaning you will radiate with that same low energy. I felt like I was a failure because of my inability to make my dream come true. What I did not realize is that I can build a completely different reality, but it would take time. What you must implant in your mind is the fact that failure is going to be one of your greatest assets. The reason revolves around the amount of growth that it will initiate, leading you to become great.

Failure will be difficult at first, but those who overcome learn the power of thought. At the time of my failure, I did not realize that I was being built for a different, much bigger goal. Anything your mind conceives it is possible for you to achieve. If I accomplished my original dream, then how many lives would have been changed by my story? I was placed on a path to inspire people and unlock minds through my words.

Redirection by Reflection

Today, I am a writer and entrepreneur who sells books in different countries, changing the lives of people who I may never meet. I would not have been able to do that if I completed my original goal, which shows that failure is just another form of redirection, with the proper reflection. The key to radiation is knowing and understanding the invisible energy not only around you, but inside of you. I have spent many years in the present moment, building up my energy for these future interactions. When people now meet me they can sense my positive aura. Humans are the only species with a conscious mind, which gives us immense power.

Once you realize this fact, you will be able to direct energy at your own will. The conscious is connected to your brain. It can be referred to as the director, as a sergeant is to a soldier. A sergeant gives an order and the soldier follows. That is the same thing with your mind. Your conscious mind has the ability to give your subconscious mind orders, that it must obey.

The Two Minds

The subconscious mind only knows how to act. It does not know right from wrong. It accepts all thoughts as true, embeds them in your nervous system, through your solar plexus, which is located at the pit of your stomach and creates an outside reality of whatever you implanted in your mind. The way to implant desires is by using affirmations.

My life once seemed random, but that is only because I was not directing my mind properly. What does this mean? Come into the present moment. Once in the present moment direct your thoughts on a specific goal. There is a power to purposeful thinking. No matter what you feel, think or believe your reality is being influenced by what you cannot see.

Plant Analogy

Think of your life as a plant. Your mind is the soil, and your thoughts are the seeds. Every thought that you think will eventually sprout into your reality. What many individuals think is that changing their thoughts will come with an immediate shift in reality, but that is simply not true. Allow me to present to you a perspective that you may have never considered. When you cut a plant at its roots, it will still show above ground. It takes time for the plant to die and fade away so how does this relate?

When you change your thoughts, you are cutting old roots, but your reality will not reflect the change immediately. The plant, aka the bad ideas, thoughts and negativity will still exist in your reality, but that does not mean your life is still going to result in tragedies. Your old thoughts will still exist in your reality for a short period of time, but over time you are going to make the stars align.

A major key to energy is consistency. You must be consistent in your ability to concentrate on what you want not on what you don't want. When I was 17 years old, I didn't know what was going to happen. I just had faith that changing my thoughts, then taking intuitive action would transform my life and now I am here, with my mind completely clear. When you take leaps of faith, signs will be revealed that inspire you to continue moving in that direction, which will display the importance of reflection.

An awakening causes you to reflect on everything that you have encountered in your entire life. Learning about these different universal laws caused me to removed myself from society. I spent many years in my room alone. Those years spent in my own room resulted in me reprogramming my mind, which changed my frequency and vibrations. A lot of people fear solitude because it causes them to face their biggest fears, which is sometimes their inner self.

When you face your fears it changes who you are at the roots. The roots are going to affect who and what you attract into your life. At the root is where all problems are. At the root is where all your successes begin. If you don't take the time to rid the damage roots, then your life is going to be a repeated succession of the failures that you have encountered up to this moment.

Foundation of Greatness

Concentration is the foundation of greatness. All legends know the power of presence and using their current to determine their future. In other words, your current is just a manifestation of your past thoughts and actions. Your future is just a manifestation of your current thoughts and actions. If you are not concentrating your forces with purpose, then you're not planting the correct seeds into the universe. Do you want your life to be random or do you want to take control?

At a young age, I wanted to know the secrets that influence greatness. How do you change your life when you don't have the money or connections to do so? The first step is concentration. In order to concentrate you must be definite in your goal so your soul can know where to go. The second step is to take a pen and write out your desires. Concentration is taking a vision and putting it to paper.

Writing is an important step to manifestation. When you document your thoughts, it is the equivalent to materializing your mind. A lot of people don't realize the power that comes from words. But let me ask you something. What is one of the most powerful things on this earth?

Words Never Die

Religion is one of the most powerful entities this world will ever see. Holy books have been around for generations and have influenced many great individuals. Religion was here before science and some suggest that it even influenced the field of science. Holy books have been around for thousands of years, inspiring generations of greatness. What does this mean? This means that words never die. They will always be alive.

Direct your thoughts with purpose. Document your thoughts and overtime you will see that it is worth it. What that is going to do is give your subconscious mind direction. When the subconscious mind has direction it makes leaps of faith easier to take. When you act out of faith it activates your sixth sense and intuition.

In life you don't need to know what is going to happen next, you just have to be confident in taking action. When your intuition is active that means you are discovering wisdom and knowledge through unusual forms of reasoning. Your sixth sense isn't what you see, but what you feel. In other words, leaps of faith will create experiences that put you in the correct positions, but it will be up to you to make the right decision.

Once you understand who you are at a biological and psychological level it makes life easier to live. The human body is made up of many different things, but I'll tell you two parts that you must become familiar with right now if you want to change your life. Your conscious mind, the mind that you are consciously focusing with to read these words is connected to your brain, but your subconscious mind, the mind that is pumping your heart is connected to your solar plexus, which is located at the pit of your stomach.

Electricity Circuit

Now, the solar plexus is connected to your nervous system, which is basically an electricity circuit that runs throughout your body. What that means is that your subconscious mind influences the energy that radiates and attracts. When you encounter someone who does not have good intentions, you can sense that because of the subconscious communication that you are unconsciously having with them.

When people are genuine, then you can sense a certain energy about them because of the energy that they're casting. A lot of people spend too much time focusing on the physical. The material is just a distraction. Humans are blinded by their senses, which causes limitations.

Because our subconscious mind is connected to our nervous system, we must infuse our thoughts with positive emotions. What those emotions are going to do is send out signals to the rest of the world that literally vibrate and radiate messages to other people subconsciously. That is why it is important to walk with purpose.

A purpose awakening happens when you discover your calling. When I found my purpose, I was confused. I was forced to look at life in a perspective that I had never considered. I no longer wanted to strive for material, but create an energy within that attracted everything that I desired. Do you know what it is like to want to recreate your whole entire life?

I saw potential in my gift and wanted to take my natural talent to the next level. How do you go from average to great? You must unlock your mind so that you can become more free. When you realize that your mind is precious, you understand why it is important not to neglect it.

Solitude Brings Peace

The reason I separated myself from society, over the years is because I was afraid to have outside influences affect my spiritual growth. Without realization the smallest things can affect your vibration. If you vibrate at a low rate then many things will be at stake. Do you know what it is like to desire to be great? I wanted to live my life a certain way, which is why I had to separate.

In the beginning it is going to be difficult to make sacrifices, but as time goes on you will learn the importance. The longer that you live your life, the way you're living it, the longer you are going to continue on the same path that you are on. That is why growth is so important. Growth should always be the objective, no matter what situation you are in.

What growth does is force you to step outside of your comfort zone. Once that is done, it opens possibilities that you once could not see. If you are comfortable with being uncomfortable, then you will evolve into the person that you are meant to be. That is another key to recreating your own reality.

Comfortable with Uncomfortable

When I decided to release *First in the Family* it created doubt in me, but I immediately shifted my mind's perspective. Opening up to people you have never met is uncomfortable especially when you have abandonment issues. I was not sure how people would receive my message, but people are now going to respect it because I have put in the time. If I would have never faced my fears I would not be here, in my dreams, showing you that it is possible to achieve whatever your mind conceives.

Concentration is so undervalued in our society. People want things right away. People focus on things they don't want more than things they do want. That is why presence is so important. Why do you think prayer is so important? Why do you think meditation is promoted in so many different religions and practices?

Enter Present Moment

The present allows you to increase your energy, by using thoughts to reconstruct your life. The day I discovered this power, my life changed. I began to write and read every day. If you read and write for hours it will force you to enter the present moment. The present moment builds your concentration, which enhances your energy. The more energy that you have within, means the more energy you are going to radiate outwardly with. That is how you begin the law of attraction. The law of attraction works, but it takes time combined with action.

Many people don't want to put in the time and even fewer are afraid to take action. People will go 10+ years thinking of everything that they don't want, come across the law of attraction and positive thinking and want their life to change in 30 minutes. The secret is understanding that the amount of years that you spent filling your mind with bad thoughts is the amount of years that it will take to wash away that same reality that was built upon those tragedies.

I have spent five plus years rewiring my mind, collecting my thoughts, and reading hundreds of books before I emerged out into the world. The shocking thing is that I am still in the beginning stages of my process. It will take another five or more years to erase what I built my life upon, before discovering these methods.

Water Your Seeds

If you want to change your life, understand that this book is only a sign. You will need to continue doing your own research. This book is only going to plant seeds in your mind that help you reach the next level on your journey. If you don't water these seeds they will lie dormant in your mind.

How do you water the seeds? You must pray every day. You must write out your future. You must educate yourself. You must force yourself to learn new skills and information. That is the underlying key to greatness.

I'm only 22 years old. I just graduated college and I have connected with people all around the world. When people meet me today, they do not see the process, only the product. They didn't see my transformation or sacrifices. For many years I battled many demons, leading me to years of searching for reason.

Your vision is going to require many years of sacrifice. Concentrating your attention is going to be difficult at first, but over time the amount of time that you are able to focus is going to increase. You may only be able to read for 10 minutes at first, but with conscious effort that number is going to increase. Over time, the amount of time that you are able to invest in your future self is going to increase. The reason will be due to the positive shifts that occur in your life. You may lose friends, money and hope, but that is only setting you up for something greater.

Control Your Energy

Great things must be broken down, to be built back up. Our world is made of energy and energy takes time to increase or decrease. The way to change your energy is by fixing your roots. Your roots begin with your thoughts. I cannot emphasize this enough. Where you are today is a direct reflection of what you have been thinking your whole life. It has led you up to where you are today.

If you're happy with who you are, now you have the science to improve your life even more. If you aren't happy with your life, now you have the science to rewire your brain. It is not going to happen over a period of days, but over a period of years. You are radiating with a certain frequency right now, and you were attracted to me because your life is in the process of changing. Your world and reality is in the process of reconstructing itself. Now that you have received *The Ancient Key*, you have enough power to change your reality and create you destiny.

"If we live around energy then with directed thought we can create synergy."

-Ken Viñales

6

Imagination

Magic of Life

We humans have something that no other species has. That something is called imagination. The magic of life is that we are able to create whatever life we want through our imagination faculty. What's so special about our mind is we can create any image we want, with our imagination and become it. All that is require is action plus patience.

As a human you can forget about the person you are today, forget about the person you used to be and become that person you see in the future. The number one thing is asking yourself what is required. What do you have to sacrifice in order to live a better life? The imaginative faculty is the greatest gift we have. All physical things came to be through the process of imagination.

Has it ever occurred to you that this is the only life that we have to live? That final breath that you take will be it. There is no coming back once we are gone. Why not live life to the fullest? What is the point in settling for average? The world is set up to shoot down your dreams. Being average is common.

People are designed to not believe in you. People around you will tell you that your dream is not possible simply because they don't believe in themselves. What you need to know is that doubter do not have the capability to see at the same frequency, that is why they are incapable of believing. That dream that you have in your mind is possible.

Before emerging into the world I took time away from society. When you are surrounded by individuals who are uncertain of themselves it can affect your vision. When you are destined for greatness there will be detours in place, but do not allow that to discourage you. The rise to the top is not easy. Sometimes you will have to take a step back from everyone!

Are you wondering how I knew this gift was my ticket? With this gift, came my purpose so I knew beginning this journey would be worth it. In my opinion there is nothing better than finding your purpose. Purpose is the doorway to prosperity. Prosperity is where wealth, peace and freedom exist.

Seeing is Believing

We all have some gift within, something that no one can do better than us. Shortly after discovering my purpose there were some doubts, but one situation caused me to take control of my own reality. Imagination is not taught in any institution, but it has led to the greatest inventions. When you imagine who you want to be, before ever becoming it, it is hard for other people in the world to see.

My life changed after a conversation with an old manager, during my junior year of college. The thing about working a regular nine to five is that dreamers are not appreciated for their internal greatness. Environment plays a large role in success and small minds tend to neglect, rather than show respect. I knew that I didn't want to live from check to check so I had to activate my imagination to create my future.

The thing about building a vision is that many people are going to doubt you in the beginning. I worked many years in a restaurant as a server, which can be a toxic work environment. People choose that industry because they want quick day to day money. I was making a lot of money as a young teen, but it was not my dream. The people around me didn't understand that I was in the process of creating a master plan. Do you know what it is like for someone to question your dream?

Blind Puppets

One day while at work my manager asked me, "who do you think you are to do that?" The original reaction for me was shock. When I first created *The Ancient Key*, my initial decision was to tell everyone around me. By the responses that I received it was clear that no one in my vicinity believed, except for close friends and family.

The crazy thing about society is that people who are closed minded feel as though they are helping you, by discouraging you, but that is far from the truth. When he proceeded to tell me, that he was only trying to help me it only fueled a fire within. As I reflect today, his words did help me in a positive way, but that was not his original intention.

Every day I used my imagination to construct this vision that is now here in front of you. It was hard having to tell people what I was going to do because people have a hard time believing in what they cannot see. I knew my life would be different, but not many people understood the magnitude of my brave decisions.

When people don't believe it is very easy to see. They ask questions that create emotions of doubt. How are you so sure? What if your plan doesn't work? You don't think that has been done before? Do you know what it feels like to be doubted by the people around you?

Unforeseen Doubt

When people are asking questions like that, they are sending doubts subliminally. Thoughts create emotions and emotions create actions. People don't realize that asking a question can lead to a thought, which creates a negative emotion, leading to a negative outside action. That is what used to happen to me as an adolescent.

People would question my ability to play in the NBA. What that did was cause me to rethink my plan, but as a kid I did not understand the true power of the mind. If I could go back, I would not have had to experience any regret because of my understanding of the mind and consistency. The point is that, when you are around people who do not understand the vision they will send doubts without even realizing.

Think about your life today. If you are reading this then I am 100 percent positive you have a dream. Now think about the people who you have shared that dream with. Have you ever shared your ideas with people, who were not as excited about it as you are? Do you know what it is like to explain your vision to someone in different ways, but they still don't understand?

Difficulty of a Visionary

Being a person with vision in this world is tough. I have been working on this vision for over five years and my mind is still working to become clear. What I have realized it that 99 percent of people won't believe until they can see it physically. Your imagination is your power. Although other people can't see doesn't mean that it is not real.

Have you ever tried explaining colors to a blind person? That question changed my entire perspective on life. That is when I accepted the fact; few people will understand you. Do you know how many times I have been called crazy? Do you know how many people think I am weird?

It was not easy ignoring all the negativity because it exists everywhere. Everywhere you go there is a form of negativity in existence. The truth is there is no way to get around it, the only thing you can do is transmute it. Energy is energy, which mean negative can be turned into positive. Hate can be turned into love. That is why you must trust the process, until you have nothing left.

Create the Future

Has it ever occurred to you that predicting the exact events in your life is impossible. Our imagination is a guide for our subconscious mind. We have ideas of what may happen, but even when it happens it is much different than we expected. Most of the time, our goals play out much better than expected. You see I knew this vision would manifest.

Our encounter already happened in my mind, which means the stars have been aligned. Although you weren't aware, everything that you have experienced up until this day was preparation. I could not see it any other way. When you are sure of your purpose events transpire that create an outside reality that matches your beliefs.

I tried looking at my future from many different angles, but no matter what I imagined, the end result was always the same. When you have a vision, protect it from negativity at all cost. The power is in your thoughts! Control them or you will be lost! When negativity takes control it has the potential to destroy your vision.

There will be people who do not understand your vision, but that does not mean you are crazy. It means that some are not able to view the world in the same way, that you do. At times it may be people close to you, but it is okay. You just have to build your vision in silence, until the time is right.

The Deciding Factor

There is nothing like prayer, plus patience, followed by action. That creates perfect timing. When it is time you will know. When you turn what is in your mind into something everyone can see how will anyone be able to question it? Everyone cannot be a dreamer.

The confusion comes because there are people who dream and people who wish. Do you dream or do you wish? When someone is chasing their dreams they are actively searching. They are creating a precise vision, in their imagination, using their mind. Most of their time is spent towards achieving their dream.

Then there is the opposite. People who wish vary from people who dream. People who wish talk, but don't build. People who wish do not take the necessary steps or sacrifices to manifest what their imagination has built. People who wish do not spend hours per day effectively using their imagination. Consistency and action are not part of their daily habits.

When you are a dreamer in today's society it is easy to receive negativity. People will think that your goals are out of reach, but there is no such thing. If your goals and dreams don't scare you then you are selling yourself short. In my mind, if we only have one life and death is promised, then why put a limit on anything, especially your mind?

One Life to Live

Why not shoot for the moon? Why not take what you love and become great at it? If you are doing something that you love, can you envision a future with it? Love is hope for a future. If you imagine a great future then find a way to get there. Some people will tell you that your vision is not possible, but if your mind conceives then it can be achieved.

The best way to perfect your vision is to remove all distractions. Removing distractions from my life may have been one of the hardest things for me to do. Distractions are often times your biggest temptations. Distractions may be your favorite people or activities. When you make sacrifices for the universe, the universe will make sacrifices for you.

When I removed all distractions my vision became more clear. That is what helped me realize that a blessing was near. Have you ever witnessed someone put their heart into something and fail? When you put your heart into something, the outcome will always be rewarding even if there are roadblocks in your path. Success is always the outcome, when your motives are coming from a place within.

Before the Success

Love is authentic. Love is original and has the power to turn nothing into something. When you turn nothing into something people have no choice, but to respect you. The best way to reach success is to study those who reached it before you. When I study those before me, they all have an amazing story.

The crazy thing that never goes unnoticed is that they are all just regular people. Before the attention no one knew their name, but unpredicted energy comes with attention and fame. We are all walking stories. You have a story that can inspire. The question is how can you use your imagination to separate and elevate to become great?

Think about what has occurred in your life. Imagine all the way back, up until now. Recall the good, bad and ugly things that have happened. Your life is like a puzzle and you must know how to put the pieces together.

Everything that has occurred in your life has happened for a reason, even if it takes many season to discover that reason. Something brought us together. Your past has led you here so now it is time for you to remove all fear because that is the only way to make your mind become clear.

When I discovered my gift it led to a purpose awakening. I wasn't sure when the world would find me, but I kept records of my thoughts to show people the power of imagination. I would like to take you back to a day in the past. A day after my college class where I had an epiphany. It was a day that I used my imagination to create this moment.

What would you prefer, someone who talks or someone who acts and shows the effects of their actions? This is something that I would like to show you rather than tell you. I was confused on what my future would be so I wanted to sit down and speak my future into the universe, capture the moment and turn it into a book that would inspire people after I leave this earth. After writing *The Ancient Key*, I knew that everything in my life was meant to be. Allow me to take you back to the past and show you that the power of words will always last.

October 4, 2016

It is October 4th, 2016 at 10:09pm. It has been a month since the day I wrote an intro for a book that I did not know I was writing. I finished writing that book nearly three weeks later. When I first began writing I had no clue that it would turn into a whole entire book! I did not think I was capable of writing something so long.

The first book I ever tried writing was at 17, shortly after I began reading, but I could not get pass the first page. After encountering writers block within the first few hours I stopped trying and talked myself out of it. I did not know what to talk about, but I knew there was something about my life that could inspire billions. After a few days writing a book went to the back of my mind because of my fear and doubt.

When I think about entrepreneurs most of them who write a book are already established. I am not rich or famous so why would people listen to me? On top of that I was only 17 so why would people believe in me?

That's why September 1, 2016 was so powerful. That was the day of my purpose awakening.

Today, October 4th, 2016, is me reflecting on the whole experience. There have been many negative things happening to me lately. Negative thoughts, negative people, negative outcomes and I believe it is a sign. It's tough when there's no one who really sees what you see. I talk to people and they look at me crazy.

People call me crazy because of the way I think. Do you know what it is like to tell someone your dreams and their first reaction is to laugh? Do you know what it is like to be surrounded by doubt? People have a habit of judging before they know you. I have had many people call me weird because of the sacrifices I have made for this dream in my mind.

All I do with my time now is read and write. I cut off friends. I stopped wasting energy. I am a college student, but I don't feel a need to fit in. I refuse to conform. The crazy thing is that I see this vision, but very few people around me understand the magnitude of what I am in the process of building.

The sad thing is seeing how people treat you before the material rewards. Convincing people to believe in something they cannot see is difficult. By the time the vision is manifested it is too late. Legends and icons are really just regular people, who invested thousands of hours into something, which gave them abilities that are not available to those who invested less hours.

What often goes unnoticed is that at a point in time legends could be in public without being noticed, but after materializing what they created in their imagination it is hard for them to walk into their own home. Legends know they are going to be great long before the world knows their name. How?

Great individuals develop the mindset, habits and work ethic years before. The misconception forms because it takes time for results to surface. What that means is some people won't support until you are recognized as great by other people. Since I have finished the book there has been an increase in negativity. The thing I have learned thus far is that when things start to get worse, it is preparation for a blessing.

Originally I had doubts about the book, but I asked myself *what do I have to lose?* I have nothing already. I have a dollar and a dream. Things can only get better from here. The biggest lesson that I have learned is that when negative things begin happening it is a distraction from what is being prepared.

Today was the biggest sign that the stars are about to align. While at work, I was having a conversation with my manager and I brought up my book. The advice he gave me was intended to discourage me. I told him that I wrote a book and he asked what about. I told him the only thing I know about, myself. He looked at me and told me a story. The story was about how he wanted to write a book, but realized that he was a nobody so he never went through with it.

After telling me his story he asked me so "who do you think you are to write a book?" In his mind he was helping me, but if it were not me it could have discouraged someone. A couple years ago I would have let that affect me, but I have been preparing for this. The vision I have with this book is not something that non-dreamers can see.

At this moment I believe, which means I can achieve. When I finally complete this book and get it published it is going to do great. I am saying this months and years before anyone in the world knows my name. I have the power to change the world. The plan that I have for this book is amazing. I just want to show people that anything is possible.

I believe that I am truly ahead of my time. When I finally decide to release this book everything that I spoke will manifest into existence. I do not believe I know everything. I do not believe I am better than anyone. I just know that anything is possible.

I have changed my life; it was hard, but it was worth it. I accomplished more things in one year than I did in all the previous years combined. I want to show how powerful words are. I want to show that it is possible to speak things into existence. I have written and visual proof of different things that I wrote down before it ever happened. I repeat different formulas daily.

When I go back and look at old goals I realize that I have unconsciously completed them. The future is today and I am going to find a way. I am saying this on October 4th, 2016, but when I release this message it will be many years from now.

I am not sure exactly when or how, but many people are going to be changed by my words. When I finally release my book I will sell thousands of copies of it. It doesn't matter how long it takes, even after I am recognized as great. I have accomplished things that once seemed impossible. The crazy thing is that it is only the beginning.

I am tired of aiming so low. I want to associate with the greats. I am shooting for the moon. If I miss I will land in the stars. You can see the future, it's called imagination! I just want to show the world that anything is possible. I know this is it because none of this was "supposed" to happen.

I'm going to shock a lot of people. Remember it's October 4th, 2016. Your current will be my past, when you receive this message. It's time to show people how great I am. I'm also going to show my manager that you don't have to be somebody to write a book. You can become a somebody by writing a book.

The most astounding fact about what is about to take place is that I wrote about it before it has even happened. My words have energy. My message will travel through generations. People ask me why did I choose a path that involves so much writing. My response is why not?

They talk about how boring the craft is. They talk about the difficulty to survive by it. They talk about the craft as if, it is not a craft. My only rebuttal to everyone who questions or doubts is that I have weighed all the possible outcomes.

Committing to a journey requires unwavering faith. Whether my situation is great or awful, my goal and mindset will remain the same. Some of my experiences may be undesirable, but those scenarios will not cause me to turn back. The possibility of this vision manifesting entices me more than the fear of failing. People tend to have a difficult time comprehending what they can't see. In other words, it will be hard for many to understand why I chose this path, but I can explain.

As human beings, we only have access to five senses and for those who are awake learn how to unlock their sixth sense. Five senses are what we are given to operate in this world. There are people living today that haven't sat to think about the fact; to live in this world is to do so blind.

Millions of things are happening around me, but are not detectable with my five senses. In other words, there is a type of faith needed to not only, exist, but to succeed in the world. Some see with their eyes, but what about those who see with their heart? Seeing with your heart gives you the ability to see the invisible.

I am one with words. When I write it comes directly from my heart, which passion flows. Writing activates my imagination. An active imagination provides me mystical powers. With my imagination I am able to take control of my greatness, by seeing ahead of the current moment and creating my future reality. My path involves writing because I can make a powerful imprint on the world.

I can die, but still be alive because words live forever. The power of words goes beyond my imagination because I can inspire endless generations. Generations that are not yet existing. Words paint pictures in the minds of other people. Prosperity and wealth requires giving. Giving someone inspiration also works with the universal law of returns.

Whatever energy you promote is the energy you will receive. My story will inspire millions so I will attract positivity. Inspiration has power because it creates a universal energy. When a person is inspired there is often a sense of time alteration. In other words, times seems to slow down or speed up.

When I am inspired, my senses are amplified, enabling me to access a different state of mind that remains hidden from most. There are a rare few of people with access to this realm. Inspiration has awakened my sixth sense, giving me a capacity to foresee events. This is the beginning of my journey and anyone who finds their way to me will be intrigued, compelled, following my journey to the top.

I am a master of psychology, with a passion for writing and telling stories. When you set out to do something, once you begin, there is no turning back. I will not stop. I will dedicate my entire life to writing, improving every single day. Writing has enhanced my perspectives, leading to me unlocking my mind. Not everyone has the ability to explain their thoughts with clarity, documenting their journey with precision.

People will follow me on this journey because I know exactly what I need to do to get where I am going. To get results you never had, you must do things you have never done. I am doing something I have never done, and soon blessings will begin to manifest. When this chapter of my life is complete, I will be able to come back to these words and see that I gave everything that I had.

The Present Moment

Much has changed since writing those words. College was some of the worst years of my life. I had so much confusion about myself and journey that all I could turn to was words. I began using words to give my mind a clear direction and overtime my reality became a reflection. I have formed a connection with God and the universe that cannot be fabricated and my life is going to demonstrate it.

This is the first time I have looked back at those words since writing them. As more people find me, they will be inspired by me. To see that my reality is becoming a reflection of what I created many years ago suggests the power of the mind. In the beginning it was hard to understand what was going to happen, but with faith and action magical things are beginning to happen.

It is now March of 2019 and my life is beginning to reflect my dream. The way that you take control of your life is to take time to create your future with your present moment. All you have is now. If you are living in your past then growth will not occur. If you learn how to use your past to recreate your reality, then build your future it will give will control to influence desirable outcomes.

As time goes on, even when I experience failure I do not let it affect me. The reason is due to the way I have designed my mind. When you force your mind to operate from a certain perspective, all you will attract is what you created with your imagination. I told myself I would be the greatest, now I have an opportunity to go out and take it.

> "There are universal laws, whether you believe it or not, they continue like a clock, until you come to a stop and watch."
>
> -Ken Viñales

7

Attraction

The Popular Law

There are many laws to this universe, but the one that is most popular happens to be attraction. There are many books about the law of attraction. There are many people who understand or know about this law, but how many people know how to make use of this law? When I first discovered this concept it was hard to believe because billions of people's lives consist of tragedies.

What I quickly learned is that the mistake people tend to make is believing this law is like magic. Once they discover this law, little of what they want to happen actually happens, causing them to lose hope, which make them only believe in what they can actually see. After five years of researching and experimenting with my own life, I am able to tell you that there is a cause and effect to everything that you do.

The truth is that you already attract things into your life, whether you are aware of it or not. Once you understand the science and a secret of this law, you will be able to utilize it and transform your life, along with the people around you. When I first discovered this ancient information, I was

17 years old. It seemed as though books entered my life at the right time because I was starting to feel like a failure.

The truth is that I was naïve. When you are unaware of the next event it can affect the way you move. There is something being prepared in the spiritual realm. My faith was in the future, which is your today. You must be specific in what you want. I wanted to create this moment years ago, although you didn't even know. Now you are here and my message is clear.

The key to life is not knowing what the last step is. Focus on taking the first step. That will create a domino effect, leading you to the second step. Never feed into the quick schemes. There are no shortcuts to success. Once you fall in love with the process all steps will slowly be revealed.

Broken Society

There are many books about the law of attraction. Odd are you know of this law. My question for is why are so many people living someone else's dream? This law is widely known, but very few know how to apply this concept. Have you ever asked yourself what life is?

Life isn't what it seems. We are living in a dream. People read, talk and wish, thinking that it will bring them everything they want in life. Attraction can make this happen, but it is not magic. Once it is mastered an individual can manifest any desire that grows within.

Attraction only works with a specific equation. Prayer times faith plus action is what makes miracles happen. Patience builds up energy within, which allows manifestation to occur. These universal laws take time to come to life, which is why faith is necessary. Faith activates intuition, leading to actions without fear of failure.

Self-education increases your awareness within. If I did not heighten my awareness, it would have been impossible to increase my level of consciousness. To begin a journey that will inspire billions of people you must see life from an aerial view. The difference between *The Ancient Key* is showing you how to incorporate equations and strategies into your life, creating desirable results.

The First Ever

My mind is always focused on growth. This journey is beginning to resemble a dream. *The Ancient Key* is showing you why and how dreams become realities. When I first began studying psychology, the universe, and sociology I was blind to this moment. You don't need to know everything, just believe in yourself and take affirmative action.

This message is something that the world needs to hear. There is no reason to live in fear. Fear attracts undesirable results. story It is possible to change your life, by first changing your thoughts. The second step is to effectively plan. The third step is to take action on your plan. The fourth step is to reflect, which generates wisdom and leads to growth.

If you do not learn how to control your thoughts then it will come with many cost. Uncontrolled thoughts attract undesirable events and people. When I learned about the law of attraction I immediately took action. Are you willing to change your thoughts and begin taking risk? Faith does not require you to understand what will happen. Take the leap and your life will conform around the vision you built with your imagination.

When I was 17 years old, I wanted to incorporate the knowledge I was absorbing and transfer it into wisdom. I wanted to see how the law of attraction would work in my life by applying it to real estate. Like many people I wanted to attract millions of dollars into my life so I began studying one of the most lucrative fields known to man.

In the beginning my knowledge of real estate was not great. All I knew was that understanding the game came with much benefit. Millions of people have made millions from real estate. As you can see, my original desire was money. With time my mind began to search for purpose.

Experiences are Proof

The first thing that showed me that the law of attraction was real was my brief success as a real estate agent. I was a 19 year old college student, attending a community college. A community college is a local college, that is cheaper than a university. These local colleges all students to take general education classes at a low price. The price per credit was close to 70 dollars.

Although I have a degree I am not an advocate for college. I do not believe that students should have to go into that much debt. The return on investment is never worth it. In essence, we are going into debt just to acquire a fancy sheet of paper. At a young age I intuitively understood the dangers of taking out loans so I did everything in my power to prevent that from occurring.

The first two years of college are the most vital. Many teens go away to college, with an immature mindset and fall into many traps. Traps are distractions, such as partying, drugs and bad relationships. These traps can lead to a path of confusion, which can create inner insecurities. During my first two years of college, I removed many distractions from my life. This allowed me to look at life in various perspectives.

Many people think college will provide them with the necessary tools to become successful. I was once one of those people. Now that the journey is over it is easy to say that belief is far from the truth. Whenever there was extra time I devoted it to reading books. This allowed me to perfect my vision.

Solitude is one of the greatest things that can happen to an individual. When alone a person is forced to look in the mirror. That is when questions will begin arising. Questions can make a person more curious and inspire growth. Curiosity is one of the biggest indicators of success.

The first question that came to mind after consuming large amounts of knowledge was, *what is the point of reading if this information is not applied?* If you acquire knowledge, but do not take action it will never transform into wisdom. If you acquire *The Ancient Key*, but do not use it, then what is the point?

Action is Attraction

After months of reading dozens of books on Real Estate, I wanted to put the law of attraction to work immediately. Every day I programmed my mind to make a way out of no way. I was raised by a single mother. She became an entrepreneur, although she barely graduated from high school. Due to her difficulties in school it prevented her from going to college. My mother's ability to overcome tragedy was transferred onto me.

Inside of every human is something called will-power. Have faith to take action because any outcome is possible. The law of attraction led me to books such as *Rich Dad Poor Dad*, *Millionaire Real Estate Agent*, *Millionaire Real Estate Investor*, and other books on how to make money in real estate.

I acquired knowledge, but did not know what to do with it. What is the first step when you have knowledge, but don't know what to do? The only option is to act. Act out of intuition. Start asking questions and doing research. Learn how to use the resources that you already have around you.

Those who make use of the law, know exactly how to use the resources around them. We all have resources, but very few of us know how to make use of them. Think about your life. Who do you know with power? Does anyone in your family own a business? Is there anyone you know with information that could change your life?

Once you make use of what you already have, the universe will bring more to you. Attraction is already at work, use what you have and more things will come into your life. Many know of this law, but only few effectively make use of it. Thoughts are things and are a major key.

Thoughts can be explained as streams of energy that goes to and from your brain. The law of attraction works because whatever you think, creates a magnet. Thoughts enter the universe at different frequencies and vibrations. What you send out is what you receive back. Once you understand thoughts it is easy to incorporate emotions into this equation.

Thoughts create emotions and emotions create actions. Emotions are what we feel, meaning that is the energy that we radiate outwardly with. To make use of the law of attraction you must consciously infuse emotions into your subconscious mind, with your thoughts. When people live in fear it can be sensed. The same goes for those who are happy.

Humans emulate a magnet. We all have an aura around us that is created by what emotions we implant in our subconscious. This will create a force that repels or attracts. It will take years to change your vibrational frequency, but it will come with many rewards.

Energy Around You

Your aura can be sensed by individuals subconsciously. When you act out of intuition it will create events and experiences, that match your imagination. If you are not conscious of this truth your life will happen randomly. Your mind has been programmed. Programmed by what it has been exposed to.

Your experiences reflect the events that occur in your mind. What you are surrounded by is the law of attraction. When you become conscious of the invisible world you understand the power of programming. This will help you control the frequency that you operate at. The higher your frequency becomes, the more desirable events will manifest.

That is the power of blind control. I was taking in a lot of information on real estate. My first reaction was to act on the information that I was taking in. When you are acting out of intuition, you do not always know what will happen. Experiences will be created that match the vision that you painted with your imagination. At 19 years old, with no prior real world knowledge of real estate, I found myself in different situations, attracting certain people and experiences, which led to positive outcomes.

Action allows knowledge to be transformed into wisdom. I took a real estate class during the summer of 2015. That was my first form of action. One decision led me to attracting certain individuals into my life. I met some very important people in my real estate class that I still keep in contact with today.

Real Estate Journey

Every state has its own requirements to become licensed. In Michigan the requirements are not that hard. All that is needed is 40 hours of schooling, along with a 70 percent or higher on the state exam. During that time I was not sure what real estate consisted of. The first step was taking the class. The second step was passing the state exam, which took me four times and hundreds of dollars. Passing the state exam was confirmation.

After the third time failing I began questioning myself. To fail is to prevail. Failure can be one of the greatest assets in life. It tests you mentally, but more importantly puts you in a position to grow. During hard times, you can be forced to look inward. That will promote growth in a variety of ways.

One of the greatest lessons I learned from the process is that obstacles come with greatness. Those who are great learn how to problem solve, even when it doesn't seem like there's a way. When I finally passed the state exam, I had a license, but what was next? I had knowledge and information, but where do you go from there?

My first reaction was to begin writing down my desires and goals. I wanted to sell homes in my first year. I wanted to make thousands of dollars as a real estate agent, despite my young age. I began praying on my desires. Prayer is another way of concentrating your thoughts. When thoughts are concentrated with purpose it produces energy within.

The key is to implant desires in your subconscious mind. When desires are implanted your subconscious embeds those ideas into your nervous system. When action is taken it will attract events that are greater than imagined. Many of my achievements are ahead of my time. Inspiration led to many great outcomes in my life. Many people believe that thought is the only ingredient, but that is far from the truth.

The underlying foundation is action. Action is what makes things look like magic. Many people they wish for their desires, but how many people do you know living in their actual dream? In fact, only a small percentage of people manifest their desires into the physical world.

After acquiring my real estate license I began interviewing different brokerages. I wasn't sure what it would lead to. I wasn't even sure if what I was doing was right. I was just a 19 year old kid acting off of faith. Brokerages are companies such as Keller Williams, Century 21, etc. where real estate agents work under contract to sell real estate. I eventually want to be an investor, but I did not have that type of capital at 19. My only option was to become an agent and learn the field that way.

Agents work with different buyers and sellers to find or sell a home. I didn't know what I was doing. I didn't even know people who wanted to buy a home. On top of that, what person would trust a 19 year old with their largest financial asset? That is where the law of attraction comes into place. You do not always need to know the answers, but with intuitive action you can make magical things happen.

After interviewing dozens of brokers, I landed in a situation that provided me a great opportunity to learn. It was the very last brokerage that I interviewed with. The broker from Keller Williams looked at me and saw potential. He wanted to introduce me to someone that I could learn a lot from. This was the perfect opportunity because I didn't know much about real estate.

I was in a peculiar position because of the age group and demographics that I was subjected to. What teenagers or college students are looking to buy a home? What family would trust a 19 year old with such an expensive asset? This is just to emphasize the amount of faith that my original real estate journey required. To be honest, I initially thought that my success would be like the books I read. I believed millions would be made in real estate, before graduating college.

The broker from Keller Williams admired my ambition and passion. When I heard those words, it was confirmation that the law of attraction was at work. See, the law of attraction is always working. Whether we are aware or not. From a young age, we begin manifesting and attracting events, experiences and people into our life. Although this is true, it does not require our conscious awareness.

Attract Success Unconsciously

Once I became conscious of these various laws it gave me more control. By the end of my conversation, with the broker from Keller Williams he walked me down the hall. He would introduce me to the head broker of the largest real estate team in Michigan. His name is Mark Z and he is seen all over TV in our state. He is an expert in his field. His team has dozens of members and I would be surrounded by many individuals with more experience than me.

When I sat down with him, I had a prior knowledge of who he was. His marketing is scientific and attracts much attention. The real estate community is aware of the presence that the Mark Z team creates. Being able to work closely with a master of his field opened my mind to a whole new world. The universe is always working.

What you attract into your life is a reflection of your perception. The more I opened my mind up, the more I attracted positive events into my life. This opportunity to join a powerful team would allow me to put my knowledge to use. I was also in a positive mindset to acquire new knowledge. This is a prime example of why you must always act!

If I did not act on my ideas, that opportunity would not have made its way to me. I was interviewing brokers for weeks. I had a license, but did not sell a house. I didn't know how to sell a house. I didn't have any clients and my outlook on real estate was slowly beginning to change.

Power of Intuition

When you act out of intuition, you don't always need to know what will happen next. You don't need to know how to get to the last step. Be confident enough to take the first step. That is what attracted that position to me. That is what attracted you to me. I have become a magnet because of my action and you are able to do the same.

I joined this large team where the goal was to win. Despite my lack of knowledge and age, I was placed in positions to grow. In my first six months of real estate, I was on the phone cold-calling people every day. Cold-calling is widely known in the sales community.

Cold-calling requires you to call people for hours. The objective is to convince them, over the phone, to buy a product or use a service. Could you imagine getting yelled at every day? In the beginning it was tough, but it built my confidence up. There are levels to achieving your vision.

I didn't know that in my first year in real estate, I would be a part of five deals. I cashed multiple thousand dollar checks. That was eye-opening for me at that time. It created joy and confusion all at the same time. I began thinking about life and money in a different way. Money comes when you focus enough energy into it.

Don't Chase Money

It is easy to attract money into your life. It is easy to attract new experiences into your life. Learn how to implant desires into your subconscious. Then act on the desires you implanted. One day, during the summer of 2016, while walking into the real estate office, I lost all desire to be a real estate agent. I wasn't happy. I couldn't see a future. I wanted more for myself.

I quickly realized that real estate agents are workers as well and that was not my goal. I wanted to be an investor, but I wasn't in a position to buy homes. That day I walked away from an opportunity, that had much potential. This decision was based off of faith. I acted on my intuition and a few weeks later that's when I picked up a pen and began writing.

When I began writing, it instantly led me to peace. It seemed as though I was coming into harmony with the universe. New thoughts began to emerge. You can live out your dreams. It is possible to achieve anything your mind conceives. The only requirement is to believe. No one in this world is going to believe in you if you don't believe in you.

The only way the law of attraction will work is through action, belief and faith. What you believe in will happen. The key is to reprogram your mind through reading and writing. After that you must take action. Whether the action is logical or not, your subconscious mind will create an outside reality of your imagination.

Shift Perspective

I want to speed you up all the way until now. I have had smaller experiences with the law of attraction. The real estate journey helped inspire this moment. This moment that you are reading these words. At 19 years old, I was making more than people who have family and kids, in a legal way.

At 22 years old, I am here showing people why books and self-education are the key. I have been able to convince people in this new generation to read a book. I didn't know that *First in the Family* would make it to nine different countries, in less than three months. I didn't know that people in this new generation would sit down and read my work.

That should suggest the power of *The Ancient Key*. All great things first start with belief. I have spent thousands of hours praying. Prayer helps program the mind by implanting desires only. When action is taken out of intuition it will lead to great events in the outside world. I began acting outwardly and opportunities continue to gravitate towards me. This creates an outside reality of everything that I was thinking years ago.

What a lot of people want is for the law of attraction to work overnight. It does not work overnight. The process takes years. What I am now experiencing is a product of five years. It took me five years just to say that I am beginning. After five years this is still the beginning. As time goes on more people will find their way to me. I'm going to attract more experiences. I'm going to attract more money and ideas into my life because of the thoughts that I am sending out into the universe.

Law of Returns

What you send out is what you get back. Love is the only thing that I want to attract. That is how you properly apply this law. There are many self-help books. There are many books teaching you how to change your life overnight, but the difference between *First in the Family* and *The Ancient Key* is that you are provided with real equations and exact experiences. This information is practical.

If you want this law to work you must begin writing down your exact desires. I'm not telling you to write a book, although if that is your goal it is possible. You don't even have to write pages of paragraphs. Just know the first step to reprogramming your mind is writing down the things that you want.

How much money do you want to make? Who do you want to be? Where do you want to travel? Who you want to meet? These are basic questions that you can begin with. As time proceeds, your writing will become more descriptive and past desires will materialize into the outside world.

To emphasize the power of writing, understand that I wrote about the release of my first book before I even created the book. I shared the passage with you in the beginning of *The Ancient Key*. I knew millions of people were going to find me. Although it has not happened in real time, the stars are aligning and it is now in motion.

If you apply all of these methods correctly, your life will never be the same. You now have a universal key, which unlocks multiple doors to wealth. The key to attraction is intuitive action. Have you spent time studying the universe around you? How much time have you spent studying yourself? If you desire wealth then it is important to master thyself.

> "We live in a formless substance that is undetectable to our five senses, but it allows us to combine our minds over time."
>
> -**Ken Viñales**

8

Mastermind

Understand the Universe

Greatness is not a matter of luck, but awareness. The moment you decide to enter greatness, sacrifices must be made. Certain situations will require you to think outside the box. Many people meet failure because of their low level of awareness. If you are aware then your vision will become clear.

The universe works in a unique way. If you understand the universe, it will be easy to gain control over your life. For so many years I was blind. As I look back there is no one to blame for my lack of understanding. What can you do when you are not exposed to something?

Throughout school I always felt like my time was being wasted. When we are born our life is affected by the guidelines placed upon us. We are conditioned by the societies we grow up in. Before coming into consciousness our family is already decided, along with our environment, which has a drastic impact on our future schemas. We are not taught how to educate ourselves, outside of the environments that we are conditioned in.

Curiosity Opens Doors

At 17 years old, the curiosity within caused questions to arise. Curiosity created a desire to search for answers. Why do some people succeed, but many others fail? College made life feel more real. My future was becoming my present. I did not want to live life irrelevant. What if I told you there is a science to success?

Curiosity is the beginning stages of greatness. Great people want to know answers. Great people know how to ask the right questions. You must search for the answers. Give your mind a destination and the rest will follow suit. Curiosity helps you find answers to questions that suddenly arise.

There is valuable information in this world. Knowledge is not always utilized. If knowledge is not applied to create a new experience then it will never translate into power. These methods have been applied, creating real experiences, in the outside world. Self-education led me to discovering something that is known as ether. We live in a new generation where reading, writing and meditation is not promoted so my claims may sound absurd to some. I have spent countless hours planning for what is to come.

World Within Worlds

The greatest of discoveries come from scientists that were alive centuries ago. By reading old books I was introduced to thought power. Along with thought power, I was exposed to the invisible world that exists around us. Are you aware of the formless substance that was once referred to as the ether? The ether is what makes up this universe. Allow me to explain.

Centuries ago wise minds described ether as cosmic matter, which cannot be detected by any of our senses. What this means is that everything you are experiencing is only one aspect of the universe. Ancient information led me to geniuses from centuries ago, which created something known as a mastermind. You have masterminds that you are not aware of, but they do indeed exist.

What I found at 17 years old, would change the course of my life and eventually help me manifest this moment today. Today, as in the day I write these words and today, as in the day you read these words. These geniuses introduced me to theories of the mind that are not promoted so it was difficult for me to understand at first.

Understand the Invisible

The first book that introduced me to this theory was *Think and Grow Rich*. Napoleon Hill described how our mind is made up of the same cosmic energy that makes up the universe. I was mind blown. Being forced to think in a way that was once unimaginable can be shocking. As I digested *Think and Grow Rich*, the information continued to chip away at all of my preconceived notions.

My view towards life transformed. I went from unorganized, to setting goals for myself. My path is going to lead to creating generational wealth. The more people who join me on this journey, the more energy I will have to rise. We are living in a different generation, but there is a science to greatness.

Are you wondering why the ether is so important? What must be understood is that the ether is undetectable by our five senses. What this means is that it cannot be seen with the eyes, heard with the ears, felt with the touch, smelled with the nose or tasted with the tongue. In short, living as a human means you are blind. Your conscious mind, which we talked about in blind control, is not something that you can depend on. The sad truth is that many individuals do.

Our conscious mind is limited, and does not allow us to understand what is truly happening, in the universe. When I began to study this ancient information, I was confused. It was hard for me to understand. It was hard for me to initially see that all it takes is a precise plan. The first reaction that originated from reading was writing.

In the beginning, my goal was not to write books, but to create a plan. If the ether was real, I knew that by collecting my thoughts, it would lead to something great in the future. When you create a plan and then take action it has no choice but to manifest.

We Have a Mastermind

After half a decade, of researching and collecting thoughts, many things have been discovered. I now have a clear understanding of what a mastermind is. The term is used often, but rarely applied correctly. A mastermind is vital to success. It takes time for masterminds to combine, so patience is key.

Did you know that you and I now have a mastermind? The moment you connected with my words, a chemical reaction took place that was beyond your field of vision. The unseen is hard to understand. The thing with me is that I am not afraid to believe because I know greatness is destined for me.

I want you to look around you right now. Wherever you are, you're not. You may think there is a such thing as real, but there is not. What if I told you that everything that is physical first began in someone's mind? In other words, the invisible is what creates the material.

There is another world, that you aren't aware of, which has a greater influence over you. How does this correlate with a mastermind? A mastermind is where individuals' minds exists. It is the formless version of our mind, where thoughts and energy collect. In this ether, our thoughts attract and influence, different frequencies and vibrations.

This is where law of attraction meets control. The law of attraction works through the ether. In other words, thoughts send out signals into the universe, causing vibrations to not only radiate from you, but back to you. When one learns how to control thoughts, it gives them power to attract whatever they desire.

A master mind is important. It is imperative to surround yourself with people, who have a high frequency. Your closest friends have a large influence on your energy. A mastermind happens when two minds combine, to create a third mind, in the ether.

When I discovered this everything changed for me. I reevaluated my inner circle. Many of my friends began to fade away, except for one. If masterminds are created with the right people it allows people access new information and experiences.

Beyond Your Awareness

Our minds are now combined through the ether. There is a third, higher, mind available to you. A mastermind is not hard to understand or create. We all create them, whether it is consciously or unconsciously. Power comes when we are aware because it grants us infinite intelligence. Once awareness is heightened, it gives us control, to tap into this third mind at will.

College did not change much for me. I learned some new things, but how much of it will translate into the real world? I knew that my college degree was only a sheet of paper. A sheet of paper that can get me a job for a corporation. There is not much room for growth when working in a corporation. You're on a salary, trapped in short or long-term deals that come with penalties if you walk away.

Do you want to sit at a desk for your entire life? I didn't want to live my life that way. I researched success and discovered the secret to build a massive amount of wealth. One of the most valuable keys is networking, which is a subset of creating a powerful mastermind.

I have many masterminds. I am more strategic with the masterminds that I create. You and I now have a mastermind. Through this mastermind you can access new experiences and reach infinite intelligence. A mastermind is when two or more individuals, come together in perfect harmony.

When in perfect harmony a higher mind is created. In this higher mind all experience and knowledge exist. That allows individuals access, to a type of infinite intelligence. Books are great ways to connect to masterminds. Create more strategic masterminds to gain access to more knowledge.

The Other Realm

Ether is a cosmic energy. In other words, it is invisible and exists around us. This universe is made up of cosmic energy. Humans aren't able detect this energy. I am revealing information that is not new, but rather old. This information has been suggested in previous generations.

When I first discovered this information, I didn't know how it would work in my life. I didn't know that I would create powerful masterminds. I have tapped into a different level of consciousness, which makes me more intelligent. Masterminds allow you to become more creative and communicate with others in a telepathic way.

The most powerful masterminds that I have right now is with my brother and mother. I have an older brother who is an international basketball player. Through our mastermind we are able to trade experiences and information, without the other having to actually live the experience. Technically I am a scientist, but I still believe in God. I still believe in the spiritual world, that is why I have spent so much time studying both, and combining the two.

The Spiritual Psychologist

There are truth and lies to everything. I am a spiritual psychologist. I still believe in God, but at the same time believe in science. My mind is set up to always ask questions, but still have faith in the unseen. I believe in a higher power.

There's a world inside of our world. There's another world that is not detectable to our eyes. The invisible world has a large influence over us. When the invisible world is controlled it can make thoughts manifest. Did you know you can speak things into existence?

I graduated from college two months ago. These concepts have been introduced and applied by my close friends and family. Masterminds cannot be seen, but they do exist. For example, the mastermind that my brother and I have is worth billions. We are both conscious of the concepts, which makes harmony easy to achieve.

You must mastermind with people who you come into harmony with. On a daily basis, my brother and I tap into our masterminds. This allows us to collect new experiences and learn new information. I have taught my family about the universe. This makes it easier communicate through the universe, in various ways. Many of these ways are not acknowledged, especially in the mainstream media.

When you understand the concept of a mastermind, you will retrace many past memories. Have you ever communicated with someone without words? Did you know networking is another misused term. It is just a subset of creating a large mastermind. This is why networking can be so powerful.

Networking connects your mind with other individuals. This creates a higher mind, where each individual experiences and knowledge combines, giving access to both parties. Harmony is the key to this entire concept working. All individuals must be on the same frequency of thought.

Obtain Limitless Wisdom

What if I told you that masterminds are more valuable than any amount of money? When you are combining your mind with other people, you need to make sure that they are positive. You need to make sure that they are on the same frequency of thinking as you or higher. Anyone with a low frequency of thought can inhibit your growth.

When I began this journey, I prayed prayers every night. I prayed prayers of positive people entering my life. The less energy you invest into the wrong people, the more energy you will have. Masterminds must be created with the right individuals, who understand the importance of harmony. Wasted energy makes the destination to your dream longer. Masterminds are going to be your secret key. As you connect with people, your mind is going to grow stronger, which induces supreme creativity.

Through my books, The Rare Few University and traveling I am creating masterminds. It's amazing to see how much my mind has grown. I have only been out of college for three months and *First in the Family* has reached nine different countries. In the United States, *First in the Family* has reached 30 different states. In total, *First in the Family* has sold nearly 1,000 copies. I am also doing everything on my own, from writing and editing to publishing and distributing.

Life After Death

What people aren't seeing is that they're connecting with my mind, through the ether. My mind is always going to be alive, through the ether. People from different time periods are going to be able to connect with me, as if I were still here physically. Words never die, which means my mind materialized itself so my energy can be eternal.

I tell people that I time travel. What they don't understand is that it is possible to time travel, using your thoughts. By reading old books, it allows you to connect with old minds, taking you back to the past. You are reading these words after I have written them. Your current is my past. Your future is my current, meaning that I have had all of this planned.

I am revealing to people through my life experiences, how you can take these exact steps and apply them to your life. Don't hesitate to leave behind individuals that aren't good for you. If you begin to see life in energy and frequencies, it will shift your reality. Negativity is the enemy.

Power of Mind

Humans have been referred to as chemists. Our mind has been said to emulate a chemical laboratory. The reason is due to the chemicals that fire in our brain, when thoughts are created. If someone thinks negative thoughts, it sends negative energy throughout their body, which transfers into their reality.

I have been able to sell a book. I have been able to create an online university. I have been able to graduate college. I have two books written and published. I have been able to connect with people in different countries. I am building a powerful mastermind that people will desire to become a part of.

I began to search throughout my history and mastermind with some of the wealthiest men of all time. What you are seeing now is not a product of today, but a product of my past. I am a product of old souls and minds, that have aligned and combined. Self-education does not produce rewards immediately, but with consistency goals will manifest frequently.

These concepts take years of studying to understand. Repetition is the only way to embed things into your mind. It is possible to reprogram your mind it just takes time. Once you understand the psychology of consistency, you will begin to levitate and elevate. That will help you separate, creating a positive shift in your life.

The quickest way to live out your dreams is to sacrifice. I have sacrificed time, friends, love and money, which tested my sanity. I am doing something that no one around me has ever done. All I can do is thank God because I am the one.

> "The current moment was already created in the past."
>
> -Ken Viñales

9

Manifestation

September 1, 2016

How bad do you want that dream that is currently in your mind? Are you willing to have sleepless nights? Are you willing to go days without eating? Are you willing to give everything you have in order to achieve your dream? Accomplishing big goals is not an easy feat.

Not long ago I stumbled upon something. Today is September 22, 2016 and in the future, my past will be your current. What day is it for you now? I discovered a gift, which led to a purpose awakening. The birth of this gift was just the beginning.

This encounter was meant to be. You are receiving *The Ancient Key*, a powerful tool to control your own destiny. These universal methods will allow you to achieve anything your mind conceives. The only requirement is to believe.

It is possible to speak things into existence. People will be changed by my journey. They will want to know how it happened. *The Ancient Key* is the manifestation of a seed that was planted. This is the power of belief.

It would not be right if I did not give you my all. Shortly after completing this book, I realized the amount of potential in it. It has the power to inspire and transform billions. There comes a point in time where you have to show people. People will treat you regular until you show them how different you are.

My original motivation rooted from love. I met this girl, who I will always refer to as *The One*. She had a way of making me want to get better because of the fear she created in me, unconsciously. Have you ever wanted to be with someone so bad that you did everything in your power to make it happen?

When I met her, the energy felt so real. I was only 19, but I felt like her love was strong enough to heal. Heal my wounds and help me grow into a better man. I always wondered what it was about *The One*. She had my mind completely infatuated.

Have you ever envisioned a future with someone that could inspire? What about finding someone who you could generate wealth with? I always thought time would bring us together, but it has done the opposite. Not too long ago, she moved to New York to chase her dreams of becoming an actress and singer.

Love has a way of creating a desire in you, in a way that nothing else can. I told her we could make a plan, but it was hard for her to understand. I want more, she wants less, which creates pain inside of me. I feel like love is blinding me.

What does it mean, when the person you love doesn't want to combine their dreams? Does that mean they doubt you? Does this mean they don't love you? Every day my mind goes back and forth. As much as I want to chase, I have to stop and reconsider. What if I told you that I have found a way to elevate?

Transmutation is what allows you to transfer energy. Weeks ago there was an awakening, which allowed me to see that our encounter is in the making. When you learn how to transform love and invest it into a passion, it has no choice, but to manifest great things like magic. Instead of putting my heart into romantic love, I will put it into something I can trust, you, myself and this vision.

Think long and hard for a moment! Think about everything that has happened to you. Did it occur to you that the answers are there? Do you know how many times I have been called crazy because I have developed the tendency to put meaning behind everything. History always repeats itself.

Many people are going to ask me questions. How do I know *The Ancient Key* will work? When you give something your all you won't have anything left. Sometimes your lowest points are preparing you for what's to come. With pain comes gains. With sacrifice comes rewards.

I am taking on a journey that will require many sacrifices, but it will lead to many rewards, not only in my life, but yours. When I first entered college life was confusing. My peers were away at college, partying, taking out loans enjoying the moment. I was at home, locked up in my room reading books.

The first two years of college my life was all about books. I did not like reading, but when it comes to learning new information, I can engage my attention for hours. People are going to ask where my motivation came from, but it was a variety of things that could be deduced down to an emotion.

Failure had become a part of my mentality right after high school. I failed my goal to receive an athletic scholarship. Setbacks are meant to make you stronger. The fear of being average made me willing to do anything to become rich. I wanted to chase material things, instead of internal peace.

I was only 17, but life wasn't resembling what I wanted it to be. Would you risk your sanity just to find peace? How do people create gains from pain? What if I told you there is a precise way?

In the beginning of my journey, there was much worry. I wasn't sure if it was better to fit in or standout. Greatness requires a different mentality, which can make it hard for people to understand your reality. Unique destinations create doubt in those who have a hard time believing.

Life Changing Day

September 1, 2016, was the purpose awakening. September 1, 2016, was the day I realized I was going somewhere great. What if I told you there is a gift inside of you? There are many people who have the ability to write, but we do not write the same. There are many people who do what you do, but they do not do it the same.

I always had the desire to be great, but love created more energy within. What was hard to understand is that energy can be transmuted. Heartbreaks can lead to awakenings. When I failed my goal to receive an athletic scholarship I was heartbroken. Now I am experiencing another heartbreak, but in a different way.

We attract people in our life that are meant for us to grow. It is up to us to learn how to interpret the signs that are revealed. Life may separate us from certain individuals, but it is not always for a bad reason. An encounter happens that inspires supreme growth, creating a shift in each individuals life.

Life has introduced me to someone that will always be a part of my story. She was able to create a strong desire inside of me, which can be transformed into energy. Napoleon Hill is the first person who introduced me to the concept of transmutation. Transmutation is important because the more energy you put into something, the odds of it manifesting increases.

Who knows what will happen in life, all you can do is believe. I will always wish the best for *The One* for a few reasons. She was one of the first individuals, outside of my immediate family, to create an intense spark of inspiration inside of me. Our journey to greatness can never be dedicated to one thing, but a collection of people, experiences and ideas.

Thought is the greatest thing in the world because it can create an emotion. Emotions produces actions. One day I received a thought that created emotions of love, which led me to questioning myself. I wondered what would happen if I used my knowledge from *Think and Grow Rich* to transfer my energy into writing. I am making the sacrifice, by committing my life.

It is a few weeks after September 1, 2016. As I continue to reflect, many things appear to be tied to writing. Have you ever hated something, then come to love it? This is what reading has become for me. Reading has enhanced my mind.

Undirected emotions can be seen as energy. When you have an influx of feelings toward anything, find something positive to invest it into. Emotions can be dangerous. If energy is not invested into positive outlets then it will become negative and produce bad events.

I am only 19 years old, so there is nothing for me to lose. The only option for me is to try. Are you willing to risk your sanity in order to escape vanity? *There is something in my mind* was the first line. What you are currently reading is the materialization of my thoughts. When the first line was written the fact that a book was being written did not occur to me.

In my past, everyone has always been right. I allowed everyone else to determine my future. Having my brother, Kyle, as a mentor was the ideal situation. He was showing me the way, but I did not take advantage of it. When you believe in something for so long, but it does not happen it creates pain. The awakening of my purpose was a second chance.

Writing was always within me. For many years, I ran away from my gift. That is why I met failure. I did not think writing was a real gift. Writing has never been a field that is promoted by the mainstream media. It never occurred to me that I could live out my dreams through this gift.

My journey has taught me the importance of love, which is harmony. Harmony leads to peace. Your experiences are trying to direct you to love. The longer you run away from your gift, the further you go away from love. When you discover your purpose it leads you directly to love, which makes everything else follow.

This whole time, my desire was for people to believe in me. I wanted people to support me. The mistake that many of us make is we don't believe in ourselves. The first step towards greatness is believing in yourself. Have you ever reflected on your present moment, from a futuristic perspective?

Think about it. I am reflecting on this moment of us meeting before you ever met me. How is that possible? Thoughts can change your reality. In my life, there have been times where uncertainty ruled over me. Think about your current moment. Now think back ten years. Did you know that we would one day meet?

Can you predict exactly where you will be ten years from today? We all have some sort of uncertainty about the unknown, but the difference is that some allow that uncertainty to create fear. Others allow it to produce love. My biggest failure was my inability to receive a collegiate athletic scholarship. I was blind to the sacrifices that needed to be made.

When you see someone doing something that they love it may seem easy. If you are living with purpose, events happen in synchrony. What can you use as an outlet? Think of something positive that takes you away from reality. Dreams are real, reality is false.

Love oftentimes requires some type of sacrifice. It took failure for me to realize my faults. There were years I let pass me by, without making the required sacrifices. It wasn't until my dreams were sacrificed that I woke up. If you begin loving something too late, be surprised if you are able to keep it, not if you lose it.

For a long time I was confused to where my journey would lead. I felt like I had no purpose. Every time I looked to my right or left there were people achieving the dream, that I once envisioned. Was it something special about them or was it something wrong with me? When you get to a low point, mentally, it can affect your outside world.

When basketball was over for me there were two routes to choose from. It was either be average or less than average. In my mind, there was no other way to achieve greatness. Failing at basketball made me fear trying to reach for anything higher because what if failure was the result again?

I was one of those people who had no clue what the future held. It was nothing that I could see myself doing. The one thing I created my future around, was no longer possible. I was depressed for years. It led me to trying anything to change my life.

I began reading multiple books per week. Eventually I was introduced to *The Ancient Key*. If these words find their way to you understand that this was written destiny. I don't know when it will happen. I am not sure how it will happen, but one day my words will change the world.

Searching for your purpose may cause many to look at you strange. When you try to explain, what is going on in your mind, to someone who is not a dreamer it will do more harm than good. There are times were you must keep your goals to yourself. It became confusing because there was so much time and money invested into things that I did not love.

If real estate was not my purpose, then was my purpose in school? I came to the conclusion that much won't change after this degree. Up until today my life has consisted of much pain and failure. To say that the amount of pain that occurred in my life is worse than anyone else would be absurd. Pointing out the actual hurt is not even the point behind my story because everyone goes through something.

To say that the things I have went through are worse than what you have been through would be ignorant. When you fail at something all hope can be lost, but how do you find that hope again? Looking back now had I not made the necessary changes, who knows what my life may have consisted of, but definitely not this.

When this journey started, nearly two years ago it seemed that results would never come. When you put your all into something, that cannot be seen with your eyes, it can create fear. Do you know what it is like to see with your heart and not with your eyes? I have discovered a gift and that gift is writing. My story will change a life.

How surprised would you be if I manifested all of this? This encounter is a prime example of manifestation. When they say it all starts in the mind do you believe or do you doubt? When I discovered the power of manifestation it sounded crazy, so I can't even imagine what finally reading these words feel like. Allow me to enlighten you.

We've Already Met

Before you can live a part of you has to die. You have to let go of what could have been, how you should have acted and what you wish you would have said differently. When the last chapter of this book is complete I knew my life would be different, but I was not sure how. The crazy thing about life is that the future has already happened.

What if I told you that you have already lived and died? I am speaking from a time that we have not physically lived. How did I know you would end up here? When you connect with your highest self, it is done through love and purpose. I died inside, to come alive outside. The old me is no longer because the future me has taken over.

What if I told you it was possible to speak things into existence, long before they ever happen? When these words reach you it may be many years later. Allow me to catch you up. Much has changed since the release of this book. I knew this book would touch millions, but I didn't know exactly when.

Have you ever been sure of something, but fear of being wrong crowded your thoughts? What do you do when you know everyone around you is going to start treating you differently, but they do not know it yet?

You were brought to me for a reason. It may take many seasons, but great rewards come with obedience. You must obey the universal laws or you will fall. Fall victim to many illusions that will leave you in confusion. I have found something that only the greats understand.

Our encounter will not happen by chance, but rather a precise plan. Many changes are occurring in my life, but just know time is aligning for us to one day meet. Do you know where you are? Look around you. Now, wherever you think you are, you are not. What do I mean? I would like to welcome you to my dream, it is time that you absorb *The Ancient Key*.

Living in a Dream

It is now March of 2019, and this morning I woke up in my dream. My purpose awakening convinced me to become the greatest. I am the greatest of my generation and I said it before I became it. If you do not believe in yourself, then it will be even harder for somebody else.

How many times per day do you go into your future? Have you ever even went into your future? Do you know how to go into your future? I am not able to tell you how far ahead I am, but just know it is much after you read this blueprint. You still do not believe me when I tell you that we would connect for a reason after many seasons?

How can you tell the world about something when they cannot see it yet? When you are ahead of your time you have to strategically find a way to reveal it to the world. Coming in last place was no longer an option. One day is going to be your day. My day just so happened to be documented.

When a blessing comes you have to take advantage of it. *The Ancient Key* was a blessing, many doors have opened since releasing it. Those who once doubted me are now confused by what has been accomplished. How surprised would you be if something bigger was in motion?

Power Within You

The power of manifesting exists within us all, whether we are conscious or not of the act. When I first discovered manifestation, I was confused. This is not a concept that is widely promoted. How are you supposed to comprehend what hasn't been exposed to you?

Do you know what it is like to live your life blind? Do you know what is really going on around you? All of the experiences that you have encountered have come through attraction and manifestation, which is a result of the thoughts you think on a daily basis.

Humans are very powerful creatures. Our ability to control our thoughts dictates the levels of our manifestation abilities. You are reading these words, nearly three years later after the seed was planted. I knew that we would meet, meaning this encounter was destiny. It is March of 2019 and I am in the position to do something that no one around me has ever done.

The Foundation

I thank God for this opportunity because I understand that this is only the beginning. This is the beginning of showing people that the impossible is possible. As long as ideas are acted up they can be manifested. I had this book written for many years. For nearly three years, this moment was in the spiritual realm, waiting to manifest into the physical. I didn't know how I would introduce this gift to the world, but I found a way.

I found a way to make sure I would see better days. Now I am here to help you find and make a way, whether you are average or whether you are great. My words hold much weight because they are changing the way individuals see the world.

Manifestation is real. The law of attraction is real. Our universe is alive. The universe is always working. I found out this power, applied it, then created a story so you can try it. I have not only researched, but applied. This book was designed to open your eyes so you don't have to live blind.

The Magic Formula

Every single claim, has been displayed using exact experiences from my life. It is easy to talk about something, but how many go out and do what they claim? Have you ever gotten tired of being average? As soon as I began to shift my thoughts, my reality changed.

I researched the history, absorbed wisdom and applied everything I learned to create new experiences. I graduated from college, but it wasn't my only source of knowledge. I educated myself, which is the foundation of wealth. This information is just a modern recreation in a new generation.

In essence, I am an old soul in the modern day. I am destined to pave a way. If you say, then you must obey. In other words, don't say things if action is not taken. These methods will help you avoid a life of tragedies. After absorbing *The Ancient Key*, there will be subtle shifts in your reality!

The Making of The Ancient Key

The making of this book began during my junior year of college. At first, it was hard to see what was needed to turn this passion into a lifestyle. The ultimate goal is to create a profit in the lives of others. I researched various options, but the one that peaked my interest was self-publishing. With self-publishing all of the pressure is on me because I don't have the support of a big name company.

During my last two years of college, I spent all my time writing, reading and researching various topics. What people are seeing now is a product of five years in the making, but it is still the beginning because dreams are a marathon, not a sprint. The day I graduated college, I launched my business and website, which led me to publishing a book called *First in the Family*. I was not sure what type of reactions it would get, but I knew I put my heart and soul into writing it.

After a few weeks of *First in the Family* being published, I knew that it was something special and that it would just take time for it to reach more hands. During college I wrote over five books, but was not sure when they would see the light of day. Once I realized the potential of my abilities, I quit my job, moved to Dubai for inspiration and put together *The Ancient Key*.

I believe so therefore I will achieve. Every day I was around wealth, increasing my energy and receiving a different perspective of the world. My goal is to show people that you can turn your dream into a reality, control your destiny and make the people around you better. After four weeks of searching through old writings and adding to what was already created, I was able to put together one of the greatest stories ever told. In other words, my books are going to be some of the greatest ever sold.

Dedication

to

"The One"

Who knows if you will ever read these words, but there is something that I want you to know. Without you, this story would be much different. There were times when I was confused so my initial instinct was to write to you. I have many stories written about what could have been, but as I write these words today, I see that there was a bigger plan. You helped me discover a passion that cannot be put out. Everything happens for a reason and for many seasons I was left trying to figure out why. It took many years to understand that all encounters in life are meant to happen at the time that they occur. When we met there was a spark, which created a flame and that led to the making of one of the greats. Greatness attracts greatness, meaning that we were placed on a path to meet, whether or not you ever see. I believe in you because you believed in me, which is why I want the world to one day see the passion that you helped spark in me. There were many factors in place, but the day you came into my life I knew that we were both meant to become great. You helped me direct my love and energy, which led to a path of creating synergy. This is my dedication to you, this is my sincere thank you!

Exclusive Preview of
Spiritual Science of Success

By
Ken Viñales

Please Review The Ancient Key on Amazon!

Copyright © 2020
Spiritual Science of Success
by Ken Viñales.

All rights reserved. No part of this publication may be reproduced, redistributed, or transmitted in any form or by any means, including photocopying, recording, or other electronic or mechanical methods, without the prior written permission of the publisher, except in the case of brief quotations embodied in critical reviews and certain other noncommercial uses permitted by copyright law.

Media Information:
TheRareFew.com **Website**
@Ken_Vinales **Main Instagram**
@WiseKen777 – **Secondary Instagram**
@WiseKen777 – **Twitter**

ISBN: 978-0-9994018-6-6

Please leave a review on Amazon, thank you in advance!

First Edition: November 2020

Authors Note

I am on my third book. When this book was initially completed, it was a week before my 24th Birthday. 100 original author copies were signed and released. I began writing to help people learn their true power. Lives have already been changed by my words. My goal before I leave this earth is to write and publish 30 books. These books are independently created and self-published. There is not a team or funding behind me, only passion, vision, and dedication. I am not sure what the next 27 books will be about. I just know something is always hit when you aim and shoot. Lives have been transformed, long after I have died by these words. These words have traveled through generations as inspiration. Thank you for helping me make this vision come true.

Part 1
Elite Secrets

Why do those who excel in their field stand out? "Those" in this passage will be referred to as the elite. To be elite requires an understanding of the mind that is spiritual and scientific. Science questions everything unless there is supporting evidence, deeming the subject as a fact. Spirituality, on the other hand, requires blind faith. The invisible energy that connects you to this universe's creator is a belief based on faith.

Some scientists do not believe in spirituality, but the truth is that everything requires the use of spiritual forces. Without spirituality, the reality that you live in would not be in existence. Indeed, consciousness or God cannot be quantified, but that is why both fields' interplay produces success. How can you develop these abilities?

The simple truth is that geniuses are created consciously, although many are conditioned unconsciously. Furthermore, highly skilled individuals apply psychological laws to their life, knowingly and unknowingly. In other words, there is an exact way to create success in any field if the interplay between the spiritual and scientific world is understood. You will learn a specific science, a set of laws that will enable you to tap into the highest energy and intelligence source. How is this information different than something you have come across before?

This book will provide you with breakthrough psychological techniques to master your life and elevate your mind. The information presented was gathered and organized by an expert in the field of psychology and sociology. By tapping into this universal intelligence source, you will learn how to direct and control energy at the highest intensity. The truth is that your human brain is easy to program and very similar to a computer.

Information enters your mind as data. Data is processed by the mind, stored for later use, or materialized. The material form of data is known as an experience. The close relationship between a computer and the human mind is what allows individuals to become elite. Your ability to acquire knowledge, learn skills, and create wisdom, determines the levels you can reach in this material world. To master skills, there must be a conversion, internally, of information into organized energy.

When 10,000 hours of organized energy is invested in a specific field, it opens the door for mastery. Understand now, the elites invest much more than 10,000 hours. That is the generic number. It will not be possible to master dozens of skills in your life, which is why this next key is vital to know. Find one natural talent, then implant relevant information through encoding, which will be explained more in part four.

The process that it takes to master one skill will make it easier for you to become adept at other crafts. An array of skills that can be unified makes life easier to navigate. Exposure will reveal how to get what you need and from whom you need to absorb information. If you can master one skill, it will open up doors in other areas of life.

The secret to skill mastery is information conversion through data consumption and application. Information can be obtained through many different channels. Intelligence dictates the capacity in which you can consume a stimulus, then transform that stimulus into a real-life experience. Hence, data conversion, absorbing information to create experiences, so wisdom is extracted. When your mind takes in information, it is received as data. Just because a person consumes data does not mean they know how to yield wisdom and advance in life.

The current generation has access to something called the internet. The internet is something that people in past eras were not able to imagine. It is a luxury to have platforms like Google and YouTube, where information can be gathered in seconds—coming back to the point. Two people can have the same opportunities and resources, but the data is converted differently in each person's mind, dictating their perception of reality.

The intelligent person understands how to transform mental data, into extractable experiences, for future development. When you create an experience, what you take from that is wisdom. Knowledge consumption can be seen as a door, a door that births wisdom. When information is applied to the physical world, wisdom is born.

Wisdom is essential because knowledge or information without experience is philosophy. On the flip side, experience without knowledge is ignorance. The interplay between the two produces wisdom. Once the mind is wired for a belief, habit, or direction, it is more than likely going to transpire into the real world. As time goes on, your mind will learn how to transform data into an awakening experience for future advancement.

Take a moment to think back to the beginning days of life. Upon entering this world, each human is a blank slate. There are no experiences, information, or knowledge of the world. A lack of understanding creates dependency. The environment a child is conditioned in will have an enormous impact on their reality and future.

Over time, information entered your mind as data was stored as an experience, fact, idea, or lesson and helped you interact with the world. The reality around you is created through your experiences. Have you taken the time to study them? Your mind projects the beliefs you have adopted onto the world. Your energy and habits will attract a particular life to you, which you are currently living in.

The environment you were raised in does most of the early mental conditioning, for those form your beliefs on love, self-esteem, discipline, and many habits ingrained in you. The purpose of this manuscript is to take you behind the scenes of your mind. You will be given an exact science, set of laws, and formula to reconstruct your mind. If you are good, this will make you great. If you are great, it will turn you into a legend.

What about those who are lost? The average? If this information becomes organized knowledge, there will be no limitation in this world for you. The result will be riches. When success is studied, down to the core, what will be found is that it begins with one's mind, your mind. These laws and practices must be understood before they can be obeyed.

Many desire success. Many people speak of success. Many claim success. The question arises when life transpires, and only a small percentage of people can reach elite levels. While money, status, and power all play a role, the most important key is the master, in other words, your mind.

Those who reach elite levels have a keen connection with universal intelligence. The same universal intelligence that you are connecting with now. There is nothing different from how the mind functions, from person to person, at the primary level. What varies is the capacity of understanding that each individual has for their brain and mind. Once the mind is understood, it makes it easy to program your brain.

The mind is unique because of its ability to absorb data. Think about the number of things that do not require thought. When is the last time it required thought to walk, speak, or see? All of these basic functions activate neurons inside of your brain. What are neurons?

Neurons are cells. These cells transmit energy and information from your brain to other areas of the brain. Data is also transported throughout your body through the nervous system. Why is this important to understand? Each function previously stated requires some type of brain activity, but the sight of that is unavailable.

Neurons are vehicles of data that shape your reality through transportation. How do these neurons work? When an idea, action, or emotion is evoked, the effect is a neuron firing in the brain. Information serves as a stimulus for your mind, which can create beliefs, subconsciously instilling habits. Humans are subconscious animals. Humans are lazy, which is why you rely on the subconscious mind so much.

Imagine a piece of clay that is used for pottery. It starts as just a block or ball of clay. As the potter molds the clay, it begins to form into a vessel. Once the vessel is constructed, it is fired at high temperatures to give it a hard, durable shape, which is the same thing that happens to your brain through exposure and repetition.

Now imagine what happens if the vessel is dropped after it crystallizes. Your mind should have envisioned the shattering of a vase. In this example, the vase represents the process that your mind undergoes when it receives a powerful message or sign. This information entered your life for a reason, and the result will be a complete halt of your reality. The result will lead to a rapid increase in mental, spiritual, and emotional growth.

When the mind has a shift, in reality, a collection of things happen. The first is already underway, which begins with questioning. Questions act as a key because it creates openings that were once non-existent. What does that mean? When you ask yourself why your beliefs will begin to take on a different meaning. Subconsciously you will search for answers to questions never considered. Answers can only be found within.

Why are you where you are today? Why do you follow the religion that you believe in? Why do you love the way you love? Why do you make the amount of money that you do? Why do you want the things you want?

The "why" phase is the shattering phase because it sends your mind on a lifelong journey. An unconscious force will draw information to you. New information allows for the molding of your brain. As you uncover more details, experiences will materialize. Once your knowledge becomes an experience, the reshaping process initiates.

Your mind is like the potter, and your brain is the clay. Your brain is remarkably plastic and has the capability of being molded. Now substitute your hands for your words, thoughts, and environment. These are examples of what affects the clay; in other words, the programming of your brain. Beliefs and habits take life through repetition and exposure. Once it becomes a part of your subconscious mind, less thought is required, and the odds of a reversal are slim.

Your mind is separate from your brain, meaning it cannot be seen nor quantified. Unlike the brain, which is an organ, the mind has no true limitations. There is a unique similarity with the entire universe. What does this mean? Years of research has been done on this thing called the universe. The universe as a whole entity is impossible to imagine in the mind.

In the invisible world of thought, the only limitation is whatever you allow the limit to be. The world's elites understand the spiritual and can tap into some of the highest dimensions of thought through science. In the invisible world exists emotions, beliefs, energy, frequency, and consciousness. Deduce the invisible world down to an atom in your brain, and there will be a shift.

The same atoms that created this universe from nothingness are the same atoms that make up your organs. At the basic level, atoms consist of energy, the foundation of the universe. Your environment is nothing more than information for your mind to encode into your brain, which will be explained more in parts four and five. An essential part of encoding is attentional capture. Without attentional capture, it is more challenging to learn something.

What will empower you is the acquisition of wisdom through high information intake, followed by application. The activation of neurons transfers into your brain. When you think, act, or spend time in an environment, neurons activating transmit information.

The spiritual world is essential to understand because of the oneness that you share with it. The scientific world is vital to understand because it reveals formulas and laws that bind specific outcomes to nature. Both are more powerful together because it combines the laws of nature with the laws of the universe. What this does is provide you with a way to control reality.

When beginning a journey, there must be an envisioned destination; write it down, for which your mind will find a direction. Whatever you decided upon is what will appear in your outside reality. For this form of thinking to come to life, you must make a sacrifice. One sacrifice may be ceasing all preconceived notions or beliefs. For you to understand the mind of the elite, you must adopt the mentality of the elite.

Throughout this manuscript, facts and philosophies will be presented. This new perspective will empower you with information and knowledge. People are blind to many things; sometimes, it can be their greatness. You can encode greatness into your mind, like installing software onto a computer. You are subconsciously programmed everywhere you turn. If you do enough studying, your mind will begin to seek more truth and ask more questions.

You have been programmed. Whether you have taken the time to understand that fact or not, it is true. The real power comes when you encode intelligence for exponential growth. Since birth, your brain and mind have been under the influence of everything around you beyond your control. The environment you live in, the media you consume, the people you spend time with all shape your brain. Those variables will determine who you become, what you feel, how you think, and what you see.

As a human, you will be programmed, so why not learn how to do it yourself? Through this course, you will develop every tool that you need to experience the success you envision. Knowledge empowers you, only if you are knowledgeable enough to apply it. As you consume more relevant knowledge, a change in mind will persist. The science presented has been extracted from research and some elite individuals' minds from various fields.

From a broad perspective, the encoding begins at an early age. Some are unaware of this, as well as many other things. Take a moment to think about some of the things you may have believed in as a child. Were you ever excited about Santa Claus? How about putting your tooth under a pillow? What about the fantasies that you had during your adolescent years.

What has changed from then until now? Do you still believe in the same things? Do you still have the same excitement for specific ideas? The answer will reveal a change in your mind, but what was the cause of the change? The underlying catalyst for change will be experiencing different things. When your mind becomes aware of something it was not before, a transformation is initiated.

You cannot change what you are unaware of, which is the first step. Enhance your perspective. Ask more questions. Think about why things are the way they are. What's so interesting about the human mind is the constant activity. Even when you are not aware, your mind is always working and scanning the environment.

For instance, are you controlling the pumping of your heart? The subconscious mind is in control of your survival. In other words, your subconscious mind is always scanning and absorbing the environment. Your conscious mind is your identity. The conscious mind is what allows you to focus and produce energy.

Your mind feeds off of its surroundings. The environment is food to your mind. What your mind consumes will affect the lens that perceives life. People from similar areas have similar forms of communication, ways of life, and sources of entertainment. That truth should be an indicator of how the mind absorbs its natural surroundings.

Greatness begins in the mind. The elite have a unique understanding of science, combing it with the spiritual realm. You will learn the secret to developing this elite mindset. The Spiritual Science of Success will help you see how close you are to the top. The first step is enhancing your perspective.

New information can be hard to dissect. When exposed to new ideas, it can create an internal shock or confusion. Knowledge is powerful, but it is not equal to power. Do not get the cliché confused with real life. Organized knowledge is power when directed precisely. If information is not applied to create an experience, then it lies in the mind, useless. Internal data must become material wisdom.

Now that you are internalizing this information, it will be vital to adopt the laws and practices. Perception will play a large role. Without an open mind, it will be difficult to understand. Lack of understanding will only make the application process more confusing. In short, many practical tools will be provided.

The greater your perspective, the more aware you will become. The way to increase perception is through breaks of reflection. Reflection will allow your mind to observe from an outside point of view. Old experiences will begin connecting themselves to new information, which in turn will produce wisdom.

It is impossible to predict every event in life, but you can better grasp what happens to you if you can slow life down. In other words, with higher awareness, you will be allowed to alter outcomes with a more precise perception. This manuscript will reveal to you the secret science, which will elevate your mind and spirit.

This manuscript will expose you to research that began centuries ago. These words were not written for entertainment, rather for enlightenment. You must be an individual who obsesses over success. You must want to live your life with purpose. Last, you must value growth and accountability. No matter who you are or where you are, there is always more you can learn.

Billionaires, athletes, scientists, actors, investors, and many more have used the information presented. If you feel that you cannot benefit from what is being shared, you will not gain from what is being taught. The wise man knows he knows nothing at all. As you go deeper, your mind will begin to form new ideas while building on the existing thoughts. Welcome to the spiritual science of success.

Entire book available on TheRareFew.com or Amazon.com

www.ingramcontent.com/pod-product-compliance
Lightning Source LLC
Chambersburg PA
CBHW032232080426
42735CB00008B/814